6.00

W9-CZU-066

STAINED GLASS TOURS
IN SPAIN AND FLANDERS

BY THE SAME AUTHOR
STAINED GLASS TOURS IN ENGLAND STAINED GLASS TOURS IN FRANCE A STAINED GLASS TOUR IN ITALY
THE BODLEY HEAD

TOLEDO NAVE

STAINED GLASS TOURS
IN SPAIN AND FLANDERS

By CHARLES HITCHCOCK SHERRILL

WITH SEVENTEEN ILLUSTRATIONS AND

TWO MAPS

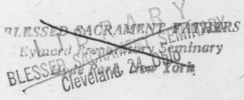

LONDON
JOHN LANE THE BODLEY HEAD, LIMITED
1924

First Published in 1924

MADE AND PRINTED IN GREAT BRITAIN BY
WILLIAM CLOWES AND SONS, LIMITED, LONDON AND BECCLES.

DEDICATED
BY SPECIAL PERMISSION
TO
HIS MAJESTY
ALFONSO XIII
KING OF SPAIN

FOREWORD

" SUNNY Spain "—colour and light, what a spell those two words cast upon the imagination, like two graceful hands beckoning us ! And if we wisely follow this beckoning and set out upon a ramble through the mediæval treasures in which Spain is so delightfully rich, what will better repay us than a pilgrimage to her ancient stained glass, where light is imprisoned in colour, where material beauty is shot through with spiritual light. And such wonderful examples ! No finer windows exist than some at Seville, Toledo, etc., and as for Leon's surpassing ensemble, one can do no better than quote a correspondent who wrote, " To enter Leon Cathedral is like walking into the glory of God."

We sometimes forget that the Low Countries were provinces of Spain during the blossoming period of Renaissance glass, and that Spain itself was then governed by a Provincial, Charles V, born at Ghent. Windows given either by that Spanish sovereign or in his honour are to be seen in all

the important glass centres of those Low Countries.
It is therefore most appropriate that mediæval
Flanders be linked with ancient Spain in these
tours, and for that purpose we shall use the golden
links of the Collar of the Golden Fleece—how,
will later be explained.

This book aspires to no more than to guide the
reader in comfortable fashion to the best old glass
in Spain and its one-time province of mediæval
Flanders. It needs no one so prejudiced as the
author to "enthuse" the traveller or to add him
to the constantly growing army of glass-lovers—
the windows of sunny Spain and war-stricken
Flanders unaided can do that. Come away then,
and store your memory's picture gallery with
windows that for years after will delight you
beside your own fireside in that far-off continent
discovered by an emissary of Spain when Spanish
glass was at its best.

CHARLES H. SHERRILL.

20 East 65th Street,
    New York City,
        January 1, 1924.

CONTENTS

LIST OF ILLUSTRATIONS

xii   List of Illustrations

STAINED GLASS TOURS
IN SPAIN AND FLANDERS

STAINED GLASS TOURS IN SPAIN AND FLANDERS

SUGGESTED TOURS

IT has long been the fashion to believe that when "the Duke of York and twice ten thousand men marched up a hill and then marched down again," they were wasting their time. In fact, the verse is only quoted after some one has done so. But did the Duke and his men really waste their time? Think of the views disclosed to them on their way up and down which would never have been seen had they remained always in the plain below and never mounted into the high places. Of course there are poor souls who never wish to go up into the higher levels of either thought or landscape. To such folk the mention of the hill-towns of Italy means nothing. But fortunately there are others for whom the word "hill" stirs the pulse, awakens the imagination, and warms the blood—" I will lift up mine eyes unto the hills, from whence cometh my help," sang the Psalmist. To such receptive ones let us appeal by announcing that everything the hill-towns of Italy or any country can promise by way of elevation in spirit and picturesqueness of site is at least equalled and perhaps surpassed by sundry cities built upon hills in Spain. Surely no high-perched town anywhere can compare in theatrical effect—dramatic beauty, we had almost said—of site with Toledo, and assuredly not surpass the assorted treasures of art, architecture, and history it enshrines. Securely stationed above the deeply gashed river that secludes it on every side, its almost savage beauty stamps your memory with all the strong outlines of an Albrecht Dürer engraving. And Segovia too, peering down from her strongly defended ridge, and Avila girt round with lofty battlements, with what proud beauty do they not dominate the landscape spread out below them ! And high-thrust Tarragona, whose lofty security of post was recognized by prehistoric cyclopean wall-builders long before the ancient Greeks and later Carthaginians and then Romans, each in turn, added to its already impregnable fortifications. As you peer down from the cloisters alongside Gerona Cathedral, you will be both fascinated and comforted by the sense of elevation and aloofness its citizens sought and secured.

But how shall we see all these alluring sights and many others beside without losing ourselves in a maze of uncharted mediævalism ? Let us be orderly in our pilgrimage, lest we waste time where there is so much and of such interest to be seen. We must first lay out a reasonable tour. Imprimis ; Spain is no country for stained glass tours planned by centuries, as is possible in France, Germany or England, because Spanish cities and shrines blossomed oftener than a century plant, so that each contains the glories of many epochs. Shall we do our sightseeing by rail or by motor ? The Madrid express leaves Paris in the evening, arrives at the frontier early next morning, and reaches Madrid that night. Certain of the Spanish highways, as for example that from Irun (at the French frontier) to Madrid, are excellent, but alas ! this excellence is not general throughout a land where local authorities decide the type of road they will build. Perhaps our best plan is to rely on railroads to transport us from one centre to another, but once arrived, turn to motors everywhere obtainable, for short trips out from such centres.

For example, Madrid, although destitute of fine old glass, affords an admirable headquarters for trips either by rail or motor to Segovia, Avila, and Toledo, respectively three hours, three hours, and two hours by train from Madrid. Barcelona is a similar centre for Tarragona, Gerona, and San Cugal, moreover it is itself still as rich in glass as Madrid is poor. Tarragona and Gerona are both two hours by train from Barcelona, while San Cugal is only a score of kilometres by road. If we enter Spain by Irun and elect to reach Madrid either by rail or motor, Pamplona, Burgos, Segovia, and Avila will be on our way. If we go by motor we will surely see all these four before reaching Madrid, but by rail it will be better to leave Segovia and Avila until after reaching Madrid. We will not advise our tourist to run out to Cuenca if he goes for glass alone, since to-day it only possesses one rose window out of all the glories of stained glass it once held. So too, we will not list Sigüenza, two hours by train from Madrid, for fine as are the three rose windows of its cathedral, they are

4

not glazed in colour, because originally of a Cistercian foundation, for which order St. Bernard in 1134 forbade the use of painted glass. The guide-books tell of its "fine stained glass," but be not deceived (as was the author). The stone barrel vaulting of the cathedral's sacristy, with over three hundred different carved heads, is nowhere surpassed in Europe, but—its glass is not stained so—peace to its Cistercian founders!

Another trip, this time by rail from Madrid, is that to Oviedo, Leon, and Astorga. By selecting a date when the express night train runs to Oviedo we may return thence (five hours) to Leon, from which it is only a short run of an hour and a quarter to Astorga. Returning from Astorga, the night train from Leon brings one back to Madrid at an early hour of the morning. The sleeping-cars are comfortable and clean, and this is the testimony of one who has recently spent a dozen nights in them! Perhaps the best sleeping-car run in all Spain is that from Madrid to Seville, which will be our next trip, not placed earlier because it is well to defer seeing Sevillian windows until toward the last, so absolute is their perfection. From Seville, we will visit adorable Granada, where is embalmed in the Alhambra the highest expression ever reached by the soul of Moorish architecture. Our glass will be found in the cathedral, and dates from the mid-16th century.

Last of all will come our trip to Catalonia, that charming land bordering the Mediterranean, where the most modern achievements of Spain vie with ancient glories. There is considerable old glass in three of the Barcelona churches, but it is more interesting than excellent, and nothing like so good as that at Tarragona or the splendid series at Gerona. On the way from Madrid to Barcelona the 12-hour railway journey may be broken by stepping off to see the uncoloured glass at Sigüenza, or at Zaragoza, from which old-world city a side trip to Huesca will show four fine old windows.

Perhaps the reader is surprised to find Flemish and Dutch glass trips in this book. Let us remind him that for 150 years the Low Countries were Spanish provinces. Some writers compute over a quarter of all the ancient windows in Spain were done by Low Country artists. And why not? They were citizens of the Greater Spain working inside the Empire, whether they glazed at Liège or Granada, Brussels or Seville. The glass

of the Low Countries belongs therefore as regu-
larly in a book on Spanish windows as does that of
Alsace and Lorraine (only taken by Louis XIV late
in the 17th century) to a book on German glass.
These incursions of Low Country glaziers, plus
the Spanish influence to-day seen in what is now
Belgium and Holland, afford one of the many
interesting demonstrations that the Middle Ages
did not need electric broadcasting to develop the
interdependence of its art movements.

And to tie this Low Countries tour to those
in the Iberian peninsula let us use the golden
links of the collar of that ancient order—the
Golden Fleece. Much too fanciful !—protests the
practical traveller. But is it ? Let him reserve
judgment until upon the windows of Belgium he
shall have seen again and again this very collar,
which even Charles V and Philip II were so proud
to wear. The rolls of the Order show many a
princely and noble name of Spain, grandees who
caused many fine windows to be set up against the
light for us latter-day folk to enjoy.

Gouda is to-day the only Dutch city retaining
a sufficient amount of mediæval glazing to attract
us, but its roomy church is a veritable bower of

softly tinted light, thanks to the long and complete array of 16th century windows. There are also a couple of fine windows in the Groote Kerk at The Hague.

If we see Gouda first and then enter Belgium from the north, we shall have a short railway trip of three hours to Antwerp. If travelling by motor, we will stop on our way at Hoogstraeten, 37 kilometres from Antwerp, and on no account should Hoogstraeten be missed, as it has the finest glass ensemble in all Belgium. The railway traveller would probably use Antwerp as a centre for visiting Hoogstraeten, Lierre, and Diest, respectively 37, 14, and 57 kilometres from Antwerp. Brussels lies only 40 kilometres south of Antwerp, a short run by train or motor. If the tourist enters Belgium from France, he will probably prefer Brussels to Antwerp as a centre for the foregoing. If he motors out from Brussels to Diest (56 kilometres) he may stop at Louvain (half way) to see some small 16th century panels in a hospital. Also, as he is to visit Liège, 125 kilometres east of Brussels, a motorist might prefer to take Diest *en route*, half way between Liège and either Brussels or Antwerp. Our nearest point to the French frontier is Mons,

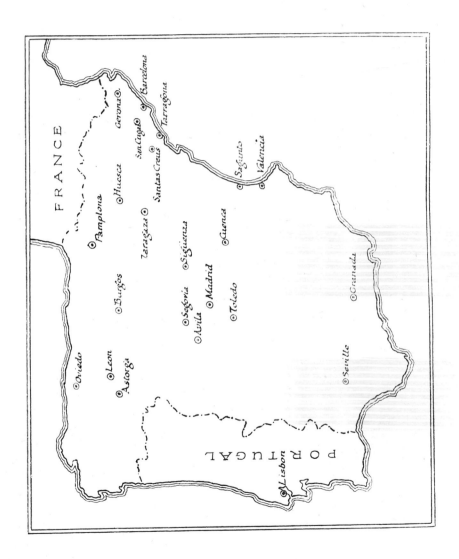

whose fine glass, although injured during the early fighting of the late war, is now judiciously restored. Our other Belgian visits will be to Tournai and Bruges, which form with Mons and Brussels an unbalanced quadrangle of which Mons-Tournai is the shortest side (about 50 kilometres), and Bruges-Brussels the longest.

If we desire to consider the cities by groups, we shall have as our first one, Pamplona, Burgos, Segovia, Avila, Toledo, and possibly Sigüenza, with Madrid as a centre. The second group will be Oviedo, Astorga, and Leon ; the third will be Seville and Granada ; and the fourth will comprise all of Catalonia, viz. Barcelona, San Cugal, Tarragona (with possibly nearby Santas Creus), and Gerona, with Barcelona as a centre. Here would also be included Valencia and Sagunto for any who care to see alabaster windows. The fifth and last group would be the cities of the Low Countries, now called Holland and Belgium, Gouda and The Hague, Antwerp, Hoogstraeten, Lierre, Diest, Brussels, Louvain, Liège, Bruges, Tournai, and Mons.

INTRODUCTION

IT is rather as a traveller, a mere sightseer, that the author bows before you, and not as one laying claim to any special knowledge of the charming craft whose product we call "stained glass." His earlier tours among French, English, and Italian glass have been meant only as guide-books, intended to facilitate and encourage the viewing of fine old windows, not only by those already interested therein, but also by others who, finding tours laid out for them all ready to hand, might thereby be induced to see for themselves the beauties left us by the window-makers of the Middle Ages. So glorious are those combinations of colour and light, that it is certain if more people could be enticed to look upon them, their inherent charm would so lay hold upon these casual observers as to make of them devoted enthusiasts.

In that spirit, let us take a preliminary ramble down the centuries without confining ourselves to

any one European country. We will cross the
Channel several times, for, alas ! like true love,
the course of ancient glass " never did run
smooth " in either England or France, Spain or
Italy, although it was more prosaically continuous
in Germany. Italian glass began much later than
the French, ripened more quickly and ended
earlier. In Spain it covered the 14th, 15th, and
16th centuries, but the period 1418–1560 covers
its best, while in Germany the craft, beginning
early, developed methodically with no serious in-
terruptions, and ended late in the 16th century.
In Spain, the development was more at the French
than the Italian pace, although it started late.

Let us begin by considering 12th and 13th
century examples of the peintres-verriers' art in
France, where those two periods produced so many
and such fine examples of their art whilst little or
none was being made south of the Pyrences and
Alps or north of the Channel.

Those artistically fruitful years were followed
in France by the dark days of the 14th and 15th
centuries, when the so-called Hundred Years'
War so long outlasted its title, and when the
constant harrying of France by English forces,

combined with plague and uprisings of the peasantry, checked the output of such artistic luxuries as stained glass windows. But, fortunately both for us and the craft, we need only return across the Channel to find in Britain's island home a veritable outburst of coloured windows, lasting all through the 14th and 15th centuries, changing its expression, however, as their architecture developed through the budding and blossoming of their " Decorated " and " Perpendicular " styles. Vigour was likewise being displayed during both those centuries in Germany, Spain, and Italy.

By the time the 16th century arrived, it is to France, Spain, Italy, and Germany that we must turn, for English glass men would seem to have shot their bolt, and almost to have ceased from practising their profession, so slight is their output thereafter. The Renaissance, so vitalizing a movement on the Continent, did not seem to show with the English such a compelling revival of art initiative as it did with the French, which, perhaps, is but natural, for the Italian wars of Louis XII and Francis I had not only shown their soldiery the ancient glories of Italian art, but had also, through the trophies they brought home with them, fired the imagination of French artists in all fields of production. Since England lacked those military missionaries of classic art, we must therefore now desert her and cross the Channel to follow our studies in France, Spain, Germany, and Italy. Again, the crossing will be rewarded by sight of a wealth of windows, but this time entirely classic and no longer Gothic in their detail and feeling. Charles V and Philip II of Spain were equally affected by the new movement in art, greatly to the advantage of Spanish windows, not only in Spain but also especially in her provinces, the Low Countries.

So markedly did the different styles of glazing alter with the changing centuries or periods, that it needs no profound student to recog- Dated nize the approximate date of a mediæval windows. window. This is especially true during the 16th century, when French and Belgian glaziers had the obliging custom of dating their work, either quite openly or else with artistic coquetry—as in the case of a window at Les Iffs in Brittany, where the date is marked on a coin held by one of the figures. This practice of dating also obtained in Spain, but to a lesser extent.

Heraldic blazons, so much more frequent in

13

England and Belgium than elsewhere, are very helpful in fixing not only the time of manufacture but sometimes even more than that, for it is the shields set out upon Gloucester Cathedral's east window that tell us it commemorates those gallant English knights who fought in the forefront at Crécy. Because the St. Edmund window in Bristol Cathedral shows the arms of Humphrey de Bohun, Earl of Hereford, slain in open rebellion in 1322, and does not bear those of Piers Gaveston, murdered in 1312, we can safely date the glass somewhere between these occurrences, say 1320. Because in one of the towers of Knole, that delightful and stately home of old England, a morsel of glazing, high up in a tracery light, shows the double bow-knot of Bishop Bouchier of Canterbury, we know that this portion of the ancient pile is at least as old as his tenancy there, which was 1456–1486.

Nor is it heraldry alone that helps us to date glass. When we visit Liège we shall know from the appearance of Count Jacques de Hern's two first wives on a window that it was given by him before his marriage to the third.

Blazons are not so helpful in France, both because their heraldry was not so precise as the

English, and also because an edict in 1792 caused the destruction of so many windows.

Destruction of glass was continually going on through the centuries, sometimes chargeable to misfortune alone, but frequently to deliberate act. The Germans near Rheims have not been the only Vandals from who craft has suffered. Aubrey's " History of Su " records that during the Reformation " one B was hired for half a crown a day to break the painted glass windows of Croydon." At Lincoln the citizens practised shooting with the crossbow at the Cathedral's windows, while at Great Malvern they quite simply threw stones at them. As early as 1330, the Commune at Assisi had to impose a fine of five lire for throwing stones at their great church's windows. When Rome was besieged by the Bourbon in 1527, its numerous ancient windows were broken up to get their wealth of lead for bullets. And sometimes peace was as destructive as war, for when Charles V was being crowned Emperor by Pope Clement VII in Bologna Cathedral, the salvos of artillery broke much of its old glass. So too, explosions at Burgos and Granada have robbed us of much delightful glazing.

Destruction of glass

At Salisbury, during Wyatt's ruthless restoration, we read that "whole cart loads of glass, lead, and other rubbish were removed from the nave and transepts and shot into the town ditch, then in course of being filled up ; whilst a good deal of similar rubbish was used to level the ground near the chapter house." It is somewhat consoling to learn that in 1632 the Recorder of Salisbury, found guilty of destroying the Creation window in St. Edmund's Church (in order, forsooth ! to let in more light), was imprisoned, fined £500, and made to apologize to the Bishop of Salisbury. After reading the boast of " Blue Dick Culmer," the Minister at Canterbury Cathedral during the Commonwealth, of his " rattling down proud Becket's glassy bones with a whole pike in his hand, when others present would not venture so high," we may be pardoned the anachronistic wish that the knights who slew Becket there had chosen Culmer instead !

Glass of the 12th and 13th centuries was made of much smaller bits than are later seen, and "Medallion" windows. because this meant, to hold them in place, a labyrinth of light-obscuring lead lines, and also because even uncoloured glass was then less transparent than it is to-day, dimly lighted interiors were the natural result. The little figures that peopled the panes in those early days were collected into groups within borders shaped like medallions, so this orderly arrangement resulted in their type being called "medallion glass." English medallions tended to be smaller than their French cousins, because early English lancets were narrower than contemporary French ones. In Italy the medallions were more varied and fantastic in shape than in either England or France. There is very little medallion glass in Spain, whose blossoming period came later than this style.

Sometimes this type is called mosaic, because made up, as is mosaic, of small bits of glass. Thirteenth century glass is famous for its Mosaic jewelled glitter, caused by the diminutive glass. panes breaking up and combining the rays of light. This was not the result of chance, for in the preceding century (12th) the pieces of glass were distinctly larger, which, of course, meant correspondingly less labour in winding about the supporting leads. Angers Cathedral is especially interesting for the glass student because there, more readily than elsewhere, he can compare the larger pieces of the 12th century windows in its nave with the tinier morselled ones of the 13th in the choir, and see for himself how the latter glisten and glitter, while the early ones show only flat colour, warm in tone though it be.

This 13th century coloured glass was stained through and through in the pot while making, and is therefore called " pot-metal " glass. Surface pigment was used only to delineate features, and occasionally to bring out folds of garments, etc. This pot-metal glass persisted later in Italy than in France, Germany, or England, and later still in Spain.

In Spain, as in Italy, there are but few examples of the 12th and 13th century epochs, so vigorously displayed at Chartres, Bourges, and Angers in France, at Canterbury in England, at Erfurt and elsewhere in Germany. A few fine ones exist at Leon, but that is about all. And yet how well suited to modify the searching sunlight of the Iberian peninsula would have been those rich but light-obscuring *chefs d'œuvres* of tiny panes meticulously joined together by a labyrinth of lead lines ! In our stained glass tours elsewhere in Europe, we have noticed that often it became

Darkening interiors.

18

necessary for churchmen to gain more light in the choir by which to read their hymn-books. At Amiens they cleared a cross-shaped space of white in the midst of deep toned panels ; at Chartres they removed a whole window of colour on each side the apse clerestory, while under English skies, French glass proved so obscuring that the 13th century glazing at York, Lincoln, and elsewhere was done in grisaille instead of following the deeply coloured windows of Canterbury's choir. Grisaille glass was made up of softly toned uncoloured panes, picked out with points of colour.

Of all the grisaille windows on the Continent, the most pleasing is a 17th century one in a chapel of Seville Cathedral. But the finest dis- _{Grisaill} play of grisaille in the world is the _{glass.} group of five lancets called " The Five Sisters " at York. That city, whose Minster alone contains over 25,000 square feet of ancient glazing, ranks with Rouen and Troyes as a " Museum City " of glass, and, like them, has many churches filled with examples from all four of the centuries when the art was at its best. Grisaille told no story like the windows of the medallion type, but, on the other hand, it did not obscure light and was therefore more practical in lands of limited sunshine. English glaziers were fond of relieving the monotony of grisaille not only with occasional touches of colour, but also by outlines of plants, leaves, or vines. "The Five Sisters" have leaves of the benet plant. There was also much fine 13th century grisaille in Salisbury Cathedral, which has a window for every day in the year, a door for every month, and a pillar for every hour—"an almanac of architecture," Thomas Fuller called it. Speaking of York reminds us that its citizens voted a tun of French wine to the Roundhead Fairfax for safeguarding their ancient windows when he besieged and took the city. No such decency was displayed by the Germans outside of Rheims, best equipped of all cities to buy immunity with wine !

A favourite French variation of grisaille is the so-called quarries or diamond-shaped (carré) panels of uncoloured glass. We shall see much of this at Barcelona. They were not only easy to lead, but also their formal designs agreeably break up the surface, especially when touches of colour were judiciously introduced, as was often the case. Sometimes, as at Barcelona, quarry windows were surcharged with gay heraldic blazons. Upon the arrival in the 14th century of the early canopies, which unlike their 15th century cousins lacked pedestals or much development above them, quarries filled in that portion of the lancet not required by the canopy. For this same purpose the Germans made use of small circular pieces of uncoloured glass, and this type of grisaille was not uncommon in Spain.

So urgent became the demand on the Continent for better illumination of church interiors towards the close of the 13th century as to develop "Canopy" a novelty called the "canopy" window. windows. During the 12th and 13th centuries French, German, and English glaziers had been accustomed to indicate that a scene was taking place indoors by surrounding it with a skeleton roof and slender pillars at the side. This is also seen on Limoges enamels, the Bayeux tapestry, and other crafts and arts of those early days—it was a widely understood convention. These embryonic roofs and pillars were destined to develop and play a great part, not only in the drawing of our subjects, but also in the manufacture of the glass and the amount of lighting it admits.

The windows of the 14th and 15th centuries

are chronicles of canopy development. At St. Ouen (Rouen) early in the 14th century, one sees pinnacles appearing above the small saints, of course in the Gothic style then prevailing. It was thus that the real canopy window began. In Spain this stage is best studied at Gerona and in Barcelona Cathedral. Notice that there are as yet no pedestals, and that the figures and their sentry-box dwellings do not yet aspire to fill the entire window space. Thus the 14th century glass designer is beginning adroitly to avail himself of this well-known convention in order to admit more light. These architectural bits were done in light tints, so therefore by amplifying the simulated stone work he could eliminate more and more coloured glass, thereby gaining better and better illumination. His canopy soon became a frank framing of his picture. There was still no perspective shown in the architecture, which is quite flat. We see but a single figure within each canopy instead of the groups which will come later. During the transition from the 14th to the 15th century styles, the canopies so far developed as to acquire pedestals and to fill the entire embrasure.

And now for what is known as " yellow stain,"

something new and very important. The canopy movement was, from its very inception, Yellow aided and abetted by the fact that at the stain. beginning of the 14th century there occurred a chance discovery, revolutionary in the technique of glass-painting. In some way (and many claim the credit) it was found that chloride of silver melted and dropped on glass, would colour the surface golden at that point. This was called " yellow stain " and was promptly employed to depict hair, to enrich costumes, etc. But most important was the effect it had upon the development of the canopy, for no longer was it necessary to lead in bits of yellow glass where needed, and therefore the simulated stonework could be far more easily enlivened and elaborated by yellow stain than was theretofore possible.

Speaking broadly, we shall remember as the chief characteristics of the 14th century period, the decorative treatment of the tracery 14th lights, deeply rich colouring, the intro- century. duction of yellow stain, the development of the canopy still without pedestal, absence of perspective, increased use of leaves, vines, etc., and lastly, shading smeared upon the surface.

Stained Glass Tours

Now with the 15th century we come to shading 15th century. which is stippled on with the brush, and in England, to increasingly lighter and softer tints, whilst an opposite tendency appears on the Continent.

In Spain there is much more glass of the 15th than the 14th century. Everywhere there will be greatly elaborated canopies. In England alone the stiffly parallel mullions of the "Perpendicular" school will spell loss of independence by the tracery lights. In England no revulsion from the dim interiors of the 14th century had been necessary, because English skies had already and long since taught the need of an adequate amount of grisaille to admit light. It is interesting to note that while the French early in the fourteenth century swung abruptly to light tints, deepening as the 15th century came on, the English (not needing the lighting reform) softened steadily from the still strong hues inherited from the 13th century on through the 14th century to lighter ones in the 15th. In sunny Italy deep colour continued throughout, and of course this was equally true of Spain and for the same reason of strong sunlight. Even though the canopy design had its usual success in

Spain and Italy, its rich colouring in both those countries shows that its success there was due to its pleasing design rather than its greater power of illumination.

We have noticed that at the end of the 13th century, the canopy became a frank framing of the picture. During the 14th century, it generally stopped at that. During the Elaboration of canopies. 15th century the canopy expanded so that not only did the simulated architecture provide a wide light border at the sides but also below, through an important pedestal, while above, the Gothic detail of crocket, finial, etc., became most elaborate. Perspective is now beginning to appear in the drawing of the canopy. In France, this elaboration of the light-admitting canopy reached such a point that at St. Lô it monopolizes nearly four-fifths of the entire embrasure, leaving but little space for the solitary saint in colour marooned in the midst of a shimmering magnificence of grey, bottle green, and yellow. These windows were presented to the citizens by Louis XI after their gallant repulse of the Bretons. At Mons we shall see a picture occupying but one-ninth of the window space, while all the rest is a grisaille frame enriched with bright heraldry. In sunny Spain and Italy, the canopy work continued to be done in strong, rich tones, although this was, of course, partly due to copying the richly hued marbles there so much employed, especially in Italy. On Marcillac's gorgeous windows in Arezzo, we see green malachite, red porphyry, polychrome marble, and much gaily coloured pavement. In Spain, these same richly coloured canopies were also very popular : in Seville and elsewhere we shall see much red used in them—a distinctly Spanish touch. Across the back of most late canopies runs a rich curtain, generally of damask stuff. This is also to be seen at Seville. During the 14th century, there was seldom more than one figure within each canopy, but large groups are generally housed in the Gothic ones of the 15th or the Renaissance ones of the 16th.

Spanish glaziers took an active and useful part in this great canopy window movement. Indeed, there are probably no more magnificent examples of this type than the richly adorned canopies brightening a dozen of the 16th century windows in Seville Cathedral, or the gorgeous circle around the dome at Granada. Some Spaniards, as at Toledo, even took the pains to make their canopies of pot-metal glass, though this meant much extra labour for leading in separate bits of yellow instead of staining with silver. Of course pot-metal glass, because coloured throughout its mass, yields a deeper and richer effect than that painted only on the surface.

This reference to surface staining reminds us that the 15th century glaziers developed and widely used another possibility of their material. A pane of this period often *Glass in strata.* had one colour on one side and another on the reverse. The French were experts at this and called it " verre doublé," or lined glass. In English, we call it " flashing." It was effected by redipping a partly blown bubble of glass into a pot containing liquid glass of a contrasting hue—for example, red into blue or yellow into red. The bubble cut open and held up the light showed the effect of the first combination to be purple and of the second, orange. This process had always been used for red glass, the thick early ruby being always thinned down in tone by a coating of un-coloured glass, lest it be too opaque. Nor were the French contented with but two layers ; I know a 15th century pane at Quimper down in Brittany that has six such layers or coats of glazing. How greatly this device enriched the palette of the glazier can easily be imagined. This system of diversifying and strengthening colour was known and widely practised by the Spaniards.

Late in the 16th century, there came into vogue yet another system of colouring, which fortunately, however, was not welcomed in Spain. This was the so-called enamelling of glass. Colour was painted upon white glass and was then fixed by firing. This greatly lessened the labour of the glazier, who no longer need concern himself with fastening into place by twisting lead lines the numerous coloured bits needed to make up his picture. This enamelling of glass had, however, two serious drawbacks. One was that where shadows were required, the glass became so obscured by paint as to lose its translucence, and the second, that in course of time, bits of this enamelled paint peeled off. This is unfortunately noticeable in Wadham College Chapel, but even more so at the north-east corner of the nave in Christ Church Chapel, Oxford. The enamelling of these paint-obscured panes makes

Enamelled colour.

us sigh for the rich pot-metal glass of the early men, who, when they needed dark tones, laboriously leaded in bits of deeply coloured glass, which gave the required shading without obscuring the light. The Spaniards were wise in steering clear of this labour-saving device.

Arrived at the 16th century we shall find Spain rich in its windows. Indeed, there is a wealth of windows everywhere except in 16th Italy and England. The magnificent century. and perhaps unsurpassed interior of King's College Chapel, Cambridge, goes far towards consoling the English for the wealth of windows then blossoming in France, Germany, and Spain, and, to a much less extent, in Italy. We now find everywhere larger scenes, more use of perspective, greater diversity of colouring, enamelling of paint upon the surface, carelessness in allowing leads to stray about instead of confining them to outlines, and classic instead of Gothic canopies and architecture generally.

And now for a word about that which may be either a kind friend or a disfiguring enemy—the lead lines which the glazier must use to The lead a greater or less extent. The author lines. believes that in the beginning stained glass windows came about because the widely popular mosaic wall decorations showed what could be done by assembling bits of coloured glass to make up a picture. If these glass pictures could only be held up to the light, how greatly the value of their colour would be enhanced ! But how to do it ? Finally it occurred to some ingenious craftsman that these glass fragments could be held together by strips of lead with small runnels at each side to retain the glass edges.

And those early folk builded better than they knew, for not only did the rays of light give life to Blending of colour. the colour they now pierced, but also by intermingling, handsomely modified all those colours. Do not forget that colour in stained glass is never absolute ! It is always modified by neighbouring colour. Blue is so radiating as always to affect nearby tones. Red, on the contrary, is light absorbing, and therefore has less influence on the shades adjoining it. For example, walk into Nôtre Dame in Paris and look up at its north rose window, a *chef d'œuvre* of lacelike stone work and design. It is purple, is it not ? And yet there is no purple glass in the window ! Thanks to the deft juxtaposition of its red and blue panes, their cross radiation yields a rich purple. This fact, once recognized, was used and developed by the late 12th and especially the early 13th century men. Here we have the reason why the latter deliberately used smaller bits of glass than their 12th century predecessors, notwithstanding the increased labour in leading which it necessitated. They did this to break up their colour, and thus to increase its interplay. In those happy days, the frequent lead lines provided all the outlines needed in the design, dark pigment being reserved for delineating features, folds in garments, etc. The later and lazier designer let his lead lines run wild, forgetting that when they did not help his design, they hurt it. During the 16th century, we often see lead lines running right across faces, figures, etc., but such extremes of laziness and inattention seldom occurred in Spain. This fact is all the more noteworthy when we reflect that the Spanish Renaissance had behind it no traditions of 12th and 13th century glazing insistent on respect for the lead lines and therefore conscious of both their value and their danger. It is fortunate that the Spaniards were more careful in this regard than their contemporaries, for their strong southern sunlight quickly reveals any injudicious use of lead.

31

The Tree of Jesse design, whose popularity endured during the entire life of mediæval stained glass, shows the vine springing from the loins of Jesse, and both the vine and its blossoms become more and more ornate as the centuries advance. In France the descendants of Jesse almost always appear as blossoms on the vine, but in England they often stand within small cartouches formed by its convolutions. Frequently contemporary portraits are used by the glazier instead of the Biblical worthies of the Old Testament. For example, at St. Etienne in Beauvais, we have Henry II, Francis I, etc. Nor was this bending of the knee to contemporary Mammon confined to the Tree of Jesse design. Upon the " Wine Press " window in the sacristy at St. Etienne du Mont, Paris, one can recognize the features of Pope Paul II, Charles V, Francis I, and Henry VIII. At Vincennes, Jean Cousin placed Diane de Poitiers among the holy martyrs on one of his gorgeous windows. Henry II, who appears nearby as a Knight of St. Michael, must have had small sense of humour to have countenanced such a disposition of his friend !

Glaziers of all periods and countries showed a

perhaps natural tendency to place along the bottom of their picture the kneeling figures of the donors. In the early days, these **Donors.** donors were modestly drawn and obscurely placed. Sometimes they supported in their hands a miniature representation of the gift window. But modesty grew less and less fashionable, until, in the 16th century, we shall find them unduly intruding upon the religious subject of the window, and in France even exceeding in size its principal personages. Indeed, at Montmorency, near Paris, Guy de Laval, the donor, occupies the entire central panel of the Crucifixion window, while at Champigny-sur-Veude, in Touraine, the care spent in painting the donors, thirty-six kneeling members of the Bourbon-Montpensier family, clearly proves how much more attention was then paid to such portraits than to the historical or religious subjects of the window. At Gouda and generally throughout Belgium the donors were evidently the first thought of the artist, while in the diminutive Jerusalem church at Bruges there appeared nothing at all but the donors. The English glaziers, however, never lost their sense of proportion in this regard. In Spain, donors are comparatively infrequent, while

in Italy they are almost never seen. Sometimes
the kneeling figures were patrons, not donors of
the window, as we shall have occasion to remark in
the numerous Charles V windows that adorn the
Low Countries' churches.

Many windows tell their tale by showing a
series of incidents. The story generally begins at
the lower left-hand corner and goes to the right.
There are, of course, occasional exceptions to this
general rule. This reminds us that opera glasses
will frequently prove useful on stained glass tours
by facilitating the study of many of those quaint
details in which mediæval artists revelled. For
example, the golden tongues of flame in the Pente-
costal window, and the Fall of Manna one at
Montfort l'Amaury near Paris, or the Red Sea of
ruby glass filled with escaping Israelites at Caudebec
near Rouen. Especially is this true of the window
devoted to mediæval sports at Leon, one of the
most engaging in all Europe. Indeed, all over
Spain opera glasses will prove useful, for the
windows are placed high up. At Granada they
are absolutely necessary.

Many were the whims of these early artists,
and one was to use tints which though inherently

inappropriate, were nevertheless so deftly adjusted to the general scheme as to be entirely satisfactory. Many a visitor to Poitiers Cathedral has gone away without realizing that in its gorgeous Crucifixion window, the cross is red and the hair of the Saviour blue. There is a 16th century window by Marcillac in Arezzo where the clouds are pink, but one does not notice it, so ingeniously readjusted is his colour scheme.

It is not generally known that stained glass windows are easily removable, and for this reason it was not unusual for them to pass on Windows removable. from one embrasure to another. Perhaps the east window of St. Margaret's, Westminster, ordered by a Spanish King in the then Spanish province which is now Holland, has suffered more vicissitudes of travel and ownership than any other in the world. On the right side, below St. George, is the only authentic portrait we have of Arthur, Prince of Wales, while across from him, in the lower left-hand corner, kneels Katherine of Aragon, his fiancée and, after his death, first wife of his brother, Henry VIII. Above her head is her badge, the pomegranate. It is probable that Henry VIII started this window on its travels just because it was a reminder that his wife was formerly betrothed to his brother. It was ordered in Dordrecht, Holland, in 1499 by King Ferdinand the Catholic of Spain and Queen Isabella as a gift to Henry VII to commemorate their daughter's projected marriage to his son, Prince Arthur, and was destined for the Henry VII Chapel at the east end of Westminster Abbey. It took five years to make, and meantime Prince Arthur died in 1502. His brother, Henry VIII, did not place it in the Westminster Abbey chapel, but gave it to the Abbey of Waltham. Upon the dissolution of religious houses in 1540, the abbot transferred it to his private chapel at New Hall, Essex, which, strangely enough, later passed to Sir Thomas Boleyn, father of Queen Katherine's successful rival. Upon his death, Henry VIII seized New Hall on behalf of Anne Boleyn's daughter, Elizabeth. Later Queen Elizabeth gave New Hall to the Earl of Essex, who sold it to the Duke of Buckingham, who preserved the glass in chests, safe from the iconoclastic zeal of the Puritans. John Olmius, New Hall's next owner, sold the window for fifty guineas to John Conyers of Copt Hall, who, in 1759, re-sold it to St. Margaret's for £420.

It is a matter of common knowledge that during the late war, many fine stained glass windows of several countries were removed from their embrasures and placed in safety. This was true of the Cathedral of Milan, of Cologne, and many other German churches. The firemen of Paris took out the side windows of Rheims Cathedral which represented the first 36 French kings and the archbishops who consecrated them. Almost all the old glass in the Paris churches was similarly safeguarded, and this was also done even so far from the fighting front as Chartres.

Of Spanish glass in general, it may be said that generally it is hot coloured, but for this the strong southern sunshine provides both an Spanish excuse and an antidote. Whatever the character-istics. reason, deep and rich and strong it undeniably is, and of a warmth and depth that would be inexpedient under the cloudy sky of England or the greys that make the French atmosphere so winsome. And those artists of the Middle Ages knew what they were about, realizing full well that the delicacy of tint so successful in St. Gudule, Brussels, would not serve under the searching sunlight of Seville, nor indeed anywhere in a land whose architects

37

have always regulated their windows both in size and placing, so as to avoid overlighting. The glowing richness of several Seville windows would lose much of their deep expression in York Minster, just as the gentle glow of its Five Sisters would admit an intolerable glare down by the Mediterranean Sea.

There is one marked peculiarity of Spanish church interiors, which, because it affects the Placing of Spanish choirs. position of the choir, necessarily also affects the lighting. This is their custom of placing the choir, not at the east end but just west of the crossing, and enclosing it on all sides but the east by a high partition. The effect is that of a church within a church. Almost always the altar is stationed at the east end, on the other side of the crossing from the choir. When a choral service is in progress, movable barriers seclude that portion of the crossing intervening between the choir and the altar, thus uniting the two. In a northern climate, this placing of the choir in the middle of the church would mean that its best lighting would be needed at that point, but in Spain, where the problem is reversed, and architects needed to modify the strong sunlight, we sometimes

38

find that windows above the choir have been blocked up. This is true at Seville, Tarragona, Oviedo, and used to be so at Leon. At Avila, and at Hoogstraeten in Belgium, all the westerly embrasures of both transepts are similarly closed to diminish the illumination.

This blocking of windows brings us to considering something seen only in Spain,—the frank filling of an embrasure with stone slabs, Blocking of only here and there pierced for coloured embrasures. panes. These slabs are generally of the same stone as the walls. In Italy solid alabaster slabs were sometimes similarly used to fill embrasures in order to reduce excessive light—as, for example, the softly pink ones at St. Miniato above Florence, the brownish-yellow ones at Orvieto, etc. This type of window may also be studied at Valencia, and at Sagunto near by. The frank use of ordinary stone slabs to fill embrasures is best exemplified at Tarragona Cathedral, which we will discuss more at length when it is reached on our travels.

Upon the use of curved stone mullions, traceries, etc., best studied in rose windows, called in Spanish a roseton, Spain has Rose much to say and can speak eloquently. windows.

Spanish rose windows began in the 12th century

with a round aperture encircled by several similar ones, generally six in number. An excellent representative of this simplest form is seen in the Sala Capitular of Sigüenza Cathedral. Then this concentric type developed into the radiating or wheel windows, usually with small columns as spokes. There are many of this second type in Spain. At Las Huelgas, Burgos, we shall see these little columns used in pairs. In the west window of San Pedro, Avila, the columns swerve slightly so as to lend an effect of revolving motion to the wheel—very curious.

It was not until the latter half of the 13th century that large Gothic roses invaded Spain from France, but the style did not long endure because unsuited to the Spanish climate. During the 14th and 15th centuries these windows tended to shrink in size. The roses of the 13th century were simple in structure, but in the 14th they multiplied their elements without, however, losing a clear sense of the geometric. It was in the 15th century that there arrived the full flamboyant type with ample assortment of elements, petal-like radiation, and elaboration of delicate stone traceries. As a variant of these more usual types one sees the Jewish six-pointed star or seal of Solomon at Valencia, at Palma in Majorca, and in the west rose at Burgos Cathedral. This occult sign was not infrequently used by mediæval masons.

So popular did this beautiful form of window become there during the 16th century that we find certain older walls were then pierced to receive the revived fashion of the roseton. A few of these Renaissance insertions are of too large proportions for the wall they decorate, notably that charmingly balanced one in the church of St. Cugal, just outside Barcelona. Generally, however, rosetones are wisely proportioned and tastefully adjusted to the wall space, nor are they so high up as to look crowded against the ceiling, so frequently the case in France and England. Nothing could be better both in placing and dimension than both the north and south rosetones of the Sigüenza transepts, albeit the Cistercian rule here unfortunately forbade colour.

The development from the early rose window via the wheel design into the later flamboyant petal effect is interestingly displayed in more than one Spanish church. Take your stand at the middle of the crossing in Toledo Cathedral : a glance down the north transept shows the earliest treatment of all—a huge round framework pierced with numerous small circular openings glazed in colour. The concentric effect is that of a group of blossoms. Turn about, and facing you at the end of the south transept is the petal effect, its lines swerving out from the centre, but with so much less stone in its traceries that you lose all sense of their support— they are lost in the design. This latter is really a window, but its earlier comrade across in the north transept seems more like a graceful piercing of an always persisting wall. In one you feel the stone wall, but in the other you do not. The western façade of Leon Cathedral has the treatment of its vast round embrasure well advanced beyond the wheel, for there the radiating lines are given added significance by saints placed around the central hub like herrings in a barrel,—logical, but of doubtful grace.

Frequently these great swirls of light and colour enjoyed pleasantly familiar names. At Amiens, the westerly, northerly, and southerly ones are called the Rosace of the Sea, of the Winds, and of Heaven, respectively. The northerly one at Chartres is called "the rose of Heaven," while

at Lincoln, the two roses are called the " Dean's
Eye " and the " Bishop's Eye."

Spain can also show us large circular embrasures
completely freed from any stone mullioning whatever, yielding one ample round space for Ojo de
a single glass picture. The Italians called buey.
this type an " occhio " or eye window, so beautifully exemplified at Florence. The Spaniards call
it " ojo de buey," or bull's eye. Spain and Italy
are the only countries so favoured. This ojo de
buey type is seen at its best in the huge west window
at Gerona and its lesser companion in the east wall,
and also at the north and south transept ends at
Seville. In passing, we must remark that Italians
were defter than the Spaniards in composing their
picture so as best to adjust it to the circular framing.
But the Spaniards excelled in their frequent use of a
smaller and modified ojo where the circular frame
is elaborated and adorned by trefoil projections
within. The circular picture inside is undisturbed,
but around it the small spaces between the trefoil
points permit graceful glazing and colour additions.
These smaller trefoil ojos are used either alone, as
in the east wall at Gerona, Tarragona, etc., or
else employed to finish off at the top a grouping of

lancet lights, as along the side walls of the nave and transepts at Toledo, Leon, etc.

At Segovia, the north and south end of the transepts show an absolutely unique type of round window. The circular space is divided like a pie cut into four wedges by one perpendicular and one horizontal stone mullion, gracefully interwoven and interpenetrated where they cross each other, and carved to represent the ribbon so popular in Visigothic and Aztec design. Rose windows of all types are so frequent throughout Spain as to furnish a special lure to a glass tourist.

If our reader be of an inquisitive turn of mind, he can indulge in the pleasing sport of tracing an Following ancient architect from place to place. For early glaziers. example, it is clear that the same man designed the stone framework of the flamboyant many-petalled Gothic roses at Tarragona, San Cugal, and Santa Maria del Pino in Barcelona. With him may have worked the same glazier at San Cugal and Santa Maria del Pino, but certainly not at Tarragona, where numerous red starfish on a white ground strike a new note in glass design. A most pleasing pastime for the enthusiast (and our windows will make you one !) is this following of early craftsmen's ramblings, for it was the fashion among those mediæval folk to wander far afield. A peculiar type of bracket supporting his saints enables one to sleuth a certain 15th century glazier all the way across southern England from West Wickham in Kent to St. Neot in distant Cornwall. Another man, this time a monk, can similarly be traced from the Thuringian Forest in Germany down through Austria to northern Italy, and probably to the Lower Church at Assisi.

Not only were the Spaniards great voyagers, as Americans have especial reason to know, but also was their own country much visited by artists from abroad. This was but natural, for so vast an Empire as that which under Charles V and Philip II stretched not only across Europe but also around the globe naturally attracted to its capital many a man whose brush and pencil sought the service of such mighty overlords and their courtiers. And we have proof that these visits were regarded with royal favour. Even as early as 1277 the records show that Alfonso X declared free and clear of taxes certain stained glass artists who later laboured in Leon Cathedral, and in 1284 Sancho IV issued an edict permitting its Chapter to change them.

The names of many of these men showed their foreign origin—Pedro Frances, Cristóbal Aleman,

Foreign glaziers.

Alberto and Nicolás de Hollanda, Arnao de Flandes, Cárlos Bruses, Vasco de Troya, etc. In connection with the last named it is interesting to remember that the Troyes windows were so widely famous that one of them, a nave clerestory light from the church of St. Jean, was demanded by Charles V of Spain as part of the ransom of Francis I of France after his capture at the Battle of Pavia. It was Micer Cristóbal the German who in 1504 placed in Seville Cathedral the first of its splendid collection of glass pictures.

Among the long list of artistic invaders the majority are Flemings or Hollanders, which is but natural, because during a large part of the Middle Ages the Low Countries were provinces of Spain. Charles V (born, by the way, in Ghent) became King of Spain in 1516, and it was not until the treaty of Westphalia in 1647 that the independence of the United States of the Netherlands was finally recognized. It was to be expected that Spanish provincial artists from what is now Belgium and Holland should wish to share in the funds then being lavished upon new glories in the Spanish

46

peninsula. We know that in 1419 the Chapter of Leon Cathedral contracted to pay 20,000 maravedis for certain stained glass, and that in 1442 Maestro Baldovin there received a salary of 50,000 ducats. Maestro Dolfin was paid in 1418 7725 maravedis of "new money" for work at Toledo. He was taking no chances with old coin that might be clipped or otherwise reduced in weight ! These and many other similar items show what attractive contracts awaited the glazier in mediæval Spain.

While it is certain that during the earliest period foreigners were brought in to glaze the new cathedrals then being constructed in the northern manner at Burgos and Leon, so quickly did this charming tinting of illumination appeal to the artistic appreciation of the whole peninsula that many local schools sprang up to teach the art. Thus were produced such masters as Juan de Santillana, Diego de Valdivieso, Valentin Ruiz, Nicolás de Vergara, and Rodrigo de Herrara. The two first named came from Burgos in 1497 to work at Avila. It was customary then, as now, for news of new building enterprises to spread widely, thus offering opportunity for foreigners to sell their skill and imagination for some great project like a church or palace. Nor were these artistic gentry necessarily unpractical—some opportunities attracted them, but some did not ! We learn from the late Juan Bautista Lázaro that when, in 1676, repairs were needed for the windows of Segovia Cathedral the authorities imposed the condition that all work must be done on the premises, which resulted in Herranz finding no one abroad or at home disposed to come forward, so a humble sacristan was obliged to undertake a task which, to everybody's surprise, he successfully accomplished. We owe much to Lázaro for his important part in the restoration at Leon, which he undertook because foreigners of the 19th century proved as unwilling to come forward as their predecessors of the 17th, since the Leon Chapter imposed the same conditions as those of 1676 at Segovia.

The pleasing illumination of certain Spanish cathedrals is enhanced by the colour of their stone. At Segovia the reddish-pink walls contribute greatly to the tinted light from the windows. In Avila Cathedral a sterner note is struck by the cold slaty grey of the stone, which seems almost to resent the glow of the glass. Inside Seville Cathedral we swing back again to mellower tones,

48

for the yellow in its brown columns and walls seems to warm the whole interior, and also tones in admirably with the faded gilding of the rejería, or iron grille work, so decorative an addition to Spanish fanes.

Alfonso X and Sancho IV headed a long line of Spanish sovereigns who were patrons of stained glass, of which perhaps the greatest was Royal the mighty Charles V. It is said that patrons. when Philip II was besieging St. Quentin, as a thankoffering for whose capture he built the Escorial, he gave orders that his artillery should be so directed as not to damage the cathedral's windows. Philip is not reputed to have been a gentle warrior, but he certainly showed more consideration for the St. Quentin glass than did the German High Command during the late war! Of course Charles V was the greatest royal patron of our gentle craft that ever appeared in any country. This will be amply proved to us when we reach the Low Countries, where dozens of windows record his name and fame. The present King of Spain, Alfonso XIII, possesses an unusual acquaintance with the stained glass treasures in his domains, and gave the author useful suggestions of places to study it, some of them unknown even to specialists in the craft.

It will be a fine thing for the cult of ancient glass when such a company as the readers of this book decide to sally forth and see for themselves the treasures herein described of mediæval colour still preserved after so many centuries for the delectation of us moderns. Words give no idea of how the originals can and will delight you. They must be seen to acquaint you with their real glories in " the bugle cry of red, the limpid confidence of white, the repeated hallelujah of yellow, the virginal glory of blue, all the quivering crucible of glass " (Huneker's translation from Huysmans).

If there be permitted a digression from the purely artistic standpoint of considering stained glass, it seems to the author that the subject opens a window out upon the field of metaphysics, something which is now receiving more of the attention it deserves than formerly. Stained glass is not merely a decoration for a window, not only an artistic supplement to architecture,—it is a manifestation of matter being interpenetrated by something not material. Coloured glass not only illumines, brightens, and

A metaphysical digression.

decorates interiors of buildings, but it has other metaphysical properties as yet but little understood. We know from experiments conducted at the Sorbonne, Paris, not long before the outbreak of the war, that glass screens of certain colours distinctly encouraged the growth of certain vegetables. Why? That remains yet to be determined. In Aubrey's "Anecdotes and Traditions" we read: " The curious oriental reds, yellows, blews, and greens in glasse-painting, especially when the sun shines, doe much refresh the spirits. After this manner did Doctor R. revive the spirits of a poor distracted gentleman, for whereas his former physitian shutt up his windows and kept him in utter darknesse, he did open his window lids and let in the light, and filled his windows with glasses of curious tinctures, which the distempered person would always be looking on, and it did conduce to the quieting of his disturbed spirits."

Here is something which one may dismiss with the slighting observation that it is quaint, or else recognize it as pointing to a *terra incognita*, as yet " not dreamed of in your philosophy." In that amazing book, " The Education of Henry Adams," the autobiographer, himself a learned lover of ancient glass, insists that the entire history of the world should be divided into but two epochs—firstly, that before the discovery about 1893 of the X-ray and of radioactivity (which period he styles the Sensual Epoch) ; and, secondly, the Super-Sensual Epoch, which, after those great discoveries, turns all our scientific investigation towards the Fourth Dimension,—out beyond the limitations of the five senses. Stained glass, considered from this super-sensual angle, affords a fascinating outlook into the Fourth Dimension, and at its very threshold reminds the sightseer that to become something more—to become a seer—he must admit that things material are, like our windows, shot through and beautified by something beyond the material, and therefore subject to other and higher laws.

BURGOS

AWAY we go then, over the French frontier from Hendaye to Irun, since it is agreed that we are to invade sunny Spain, bent on looting it to the extent of a memory full of its ancient stained glass. A wisely selected loot, this, for it will give us no trouble with Spanish custom-house officials when we leave the country. Spain has of late years lost so many mediæval treasures that recently she imposed a 100 per cent. export duty on antiques in general, and absolute prohibition upon ancient furniture. But no customs inspector, even though well equipped with an X-ray apparatus or witch-hazel rod, will discover what we have stored away in our memories, so our exit will be tranquil. To intending visitors it may be remarked that although the Spanish inspection of luggage is thorough, the inspectors wear clean white gloves while discharging their duties, a practice that might well be copied elsewhere. Nor is this the only commendable feature of travel in Spain, for the trains are comfortable and clean, especially the sleeping cars, and the food uniformly good. One of the very best travel books ever written is Theophile Gautier's " Voyage en Espagne," but the trials and tribulations he so merrily relates are of the vintage of 1840, and have long since passed away. Many read it before visiting Spain, and nervously purchase insect powder galore, nowadays less necessary there than in Paris or Berlin.

If the traveller has come through to the Spanish frontier on the Paris-Madrid express, well and good, but if he has motored, he will probably have halted at Biarritz, and that will be hard to leave. Here where the Pyrenees run down to the Bay of Biscay, is a charming resort for pleasure-seekers. It is small wonder that the Empress Eugénie loved to linger in this corner of France so near to her beloved Spain—many another sojourner has felt the same lure.

Even when the motorist is over the frontier, he may again be tempted to delay, and this time soon after leaving Irun, at San Sebastian, but to all but very serious sightseers let us whisper " Beware," for here in this engaging seaside resort is concentrated all that Newport, Bar Harbour, and

Southampton mean to an American, plus the
Royal Court in summer time. Best come along
with us and eschew the tempting company of the
lotus-eaters !

But enough of delays, we are across the frontier,
and either we have embarked in the morning
express (which left Paris the night before) that will
bring us to Burgos at about 2 p.m. and Madrid
at 9 p.m., or else we are starting by motor on the
" broad highway," which is really broad and also
good all the way to the capital. At first the road
winding through the hill country is very picturesque,
not at all like the long, sweeping, treeless stretches
which Spain will soon come to mean for us. Trees
bring birds, and birds bother crops, say the
Spaniards, so down with the trees !

Twenty-seven kilometres south of San Sebastian
on the Madrid road lies Tolosa. Sixty-two kilometres off to the left from this point, and further
up into the mountains, lies Pamplona, an ancient
city named by the Romans after Pompey the Great.
About 5 kilometres beyond it is the famous pass of
Roncevalles, 4000 feet above sea level, memorable
for many a stricken battle, chiefest among which
was Charlemagne's, sung in the Chanson de Roland.

Pamplona's 14th–15th century cathedral, one of the finest of Spain's late Gothic churches, contains along the clerestory on the north side of the nave, some four or five 15th century windows, whose delicate tints contrast with the riper tones of the 17th century panes across the nave.

But once more we are on the Madrid road. Look well upon this rugged northern country, stranger, for here is the cradle of the Spanish race. Out from these Asturian hills fought their way ever southwards a hardy people that grew sturdier after each of its long struggles for the peninsula, until, thanks to its continued training against Moslem hosts, there developed the Spanish infantry that conquered the world.

That rugged fighting spirit of the race was best exemplified in the great Cid—Cid el Campeador, the conqueror beloved of all Spaniards and born in Burgos. His spirit is embalmed in a poem of archaic language, equivalent for modern Spaniards to Chaucer's verbiage for us latter-day Anglo-Saxons. And a mighty man he certainly was, not only in life but even after death, for did not his dead body, clad in full armour and mounted on a war horse, strike such terror to the Moors as to

win a battle ! Of what other warrior's dead clay
can so much be claimed ? Now his bones, enclosed
in a reliquary in the Town Hall of Burgos, are an
object of patriotic pilgrimage to many a Spaniard.

It was from out this very town that he marched,
with but few supporters and at odds with the king.
On went the Cid south and east, fighting all the
way, always winning and adding always to his
forces after each victory. Always he sent back to
the king part of the spoils of his successful warring,
and this shrewd policy bore ripe fruit, as presently
we shall see.

On he swept, his army and his fame growing
apace, on over the Catalonian frontier and then
south until he took Valencia, and there established
his headquarters. Here his two daughters were
wed by noblemen from the court at Burgos. When
later these caitiffs deserted them in the wilds on
their way back to court because offended by their
father, the Cid claimed it as his right that the king
call a court to try these false knights. The share
of war spoils continually sent home to the king
now bore fruit, for, notwithstanding stout opposition
by courtiers, the king held the trial at Toledo.
The Cid's shrewdness in handling his pleading,

first securing return of moneys advanced and finally punishment of the two cowardly noblemen is delightfully told in Archer M. Huntington's translation of the ancient poem which he published along with the annotated original text, illustrations, and voluminous notes. This work alone would merit the esteem in which Huntington is held by Spaniards, even if he had not given New York City the Hispanic Museum, the fullest exposition anywhere existing of Spain at its very best.

It is properly alleged by critics of architecture in Spain that the cathedral of Burgos, like that at Leon, is not Spanish at all, but French. To that criticism it may with equal fairness be replied that if these two be foreign churches transplanted into Spanish soil, then that soil has in their case proven kindly favouring, for it would be hard to find their betters in the land from which they were transplanted. The placing of this superb Gothic edifice is unlike that of any other cathedral in the world, for it is thrust under the base of a hill, actually tucked in against it. A decidedly snug position for any other sort of building, but why a cathedral? So close against the hill is it, that to emerge from the north transept on to the street, it was necessary

BURGOS CATHEDRAL.   CAPILLA DEL CONDESTABLE
Glass here is German in feeling, the chapel's architects, father and son, coming from
Cologne

to construct a handsome double stairway inside against the face of the transept's end wall.

Of course Leon's peculiar glory is that of glass, but at Burgos Cathedral it is sheer beauty of architecture, for its ancient glass was almost entirely destroyed by the explosion of the Castillo powder magazine, set off by the French soldiers when evacuating the city in 1813. Almost the only exceptions to that calamity are the fine roseton in the south transept, the windows in the glorious chapel of the Condestable, and certain other isolated bits. The south rose is brightly glorious enough to satisfy any glutton of colour, no matter how ravenous—a vast pie of twenty slices, such a one might call it, for its deep and glowing hues are divided into so many wedges by the radiating mullions. In the centre is installed a large blue-robed figure, attended on either hand by a diminutive one in grass green. Round about this centre are ten circular apertures filled with deep colour, while out beyond them extend twenty spoke-like openings, each finished off against the huge encircling stone frame by a dainty half-circle of old glass. Elaborate, rich, glowing, and glorious—one of the finest rosetones in Spain. Red, a deep singing red, is the most important colour used, followed in order by a deep blue and then green, with a certain amount of brown. Very graceful too is the rose's disposition in the wall, high but not too high, and balanced below by two porticoes.

Very similar in structure to this rose is that in the west front of the church of San Estaban, higher up the hill, just across from the ruins of the Castillo. Because San Estaban was so close to the powder explosion of 1813, it suffered severely, and less than half of the old glazing survives in this rose. Curiously enough, the curve of this roseton is rather flattened at the top.

But let us return to the cathedral and penetrate eastward out beyond its apse and ambulatory into the glorious chapel of the Condestable, Gothic at its very richest. Here the architect took careful note of climatic requirements, and has placed his windows very high up. They run all round the chapel, two rows of them, eight in the upper and six in the lower, each containing three lancets. Of this total of fourteen, seven retain their late 15th century glazing. It is very German in type, especially the canopies, as might be expected since the chapel's two architects, father and son, were both from Cologne. It is rather a pity that all the old glass is not put into the easterly embrasures, so as to give a completely glazed effect to one entering the chapel from the apse ambulatory. There are also a couple of contemporary lancets high up in the cimborio over the crossing that might well be transferred hither, for they are lost and lonely where they now are.

The west rose, with the ancient seal of Solomon worked out in its stone traceries, is modern glazed, but below it, to right and left, one over each side portal, are two interesting ojos de buey. They are so flattened in shape as to remind one of the *œil de bœuf* windows at Versailles. This old glass suffered badly from the explosion, but their restoration, utilizing as it has many of the old fragments, is very satisfactory.

From Burgos we shall take two short trips out of town, one of a mile and a quarter south-west to Las Huelgas, and the other of two and a half south-east to the Cartuja of Miraflores. At Las Huelgas we shall see old white pattern glass, but none of colour, because this nunnery is a Cistercian one. There is, however, a very interesting and early rose window, of the period when small

61

columns were used, radiating from the centre. Here these columillas are in a double series, one within the other. Furthermore, the window was never glazed, for it gave light from the outside on to a porch before a door, and therefore it was not necessary to keep out the weather.

The drive out to the Cartuja is most agreeable, delightfully shaded all the way by great trees, and, as the road rises steadily, giving ever improving views out over the city below. On the plain outside the city and below the Cartuja is now installed an army aviation school, and the twisting, darting airplanes make strange neighbours for the ancient spires of the cathedral ! The chapel of the Cartuja, built by Queen Isabella the Catholic to contain the tombs of her parents, John II and Isabella of Portugal, is a long narrow edifice with no wings. At the easterly end is the noble double tomb, unsurpassed in lacy details of carved stone.

The glass that we have come to see fills all the side windows, each of three lancets, five on each side, and also the three most easterly of the seven lights that curve around the apse. The tracery lights of these latter seem to indicate that they were

CONVENT OF LAS HUELGAS, BURGOS
Marks advance on San Pedro wheel window, because more ornate and double row of columillas

originally meant to be of two lancets each, but the central mullion has been cut away.

This Cartuja glass is more interesting than engaging. It is unusual in Spain to find the old glazing so complete throughout an interior, but it *is* usual to have it possess more charm. Though not so crude as some we shall see in Barcelona, it is not excellent. The windows on the left side as you enter represent scenes of the Passion, beginning at the west with Christ at Gethsemane and ending at the east with the Crucifixion, which is the best window here. On the right are scenes of the Glory, and include Christ rising from the tomb, the Transfiguration, etc. The windows are generally of 16th century renaissance type, but if we must attempt more exact dating then we suggest that the eastmost on the right is early 17th century, while the second and third on the left are late 15th century because of their Gothic canopies.

The ojo de buey over the west portal has been robbed of its old glass so as to admit more light.

As we drive in and out of the city we are confronted by signs sternly notifying us that " En esta ciudad esta prohibido la mendacidad y la blasfemía," and it is pleasant to record that no beggars are anywhere to be seen. Why not? since begging is here rated worse than a sin forbidden by one of the Ten Commandments.

From Irun to Burgos it is 223 kilometres by an excellent road, and from Burgos to Madrid 330 kilometres. There is also another road by Aranda de Duero, 235 kilometres, but it is reported not so good. One can leave Burgos by rail at 11 p.m. and reach Madrid next morning at seven, or else pick up the Paris express at 2 p.m. arriving at Madrid that evening at nine.

MADRID

LOOK at a shaded population map of Spain. You will be surprised to learn from its varying depths of tint that most of its people live along the seacoast, the only notable inland exception being the darkly shaded tract around Madrid. And yet when you reach that city, you will find none of the physical reasons that usually make for a metropolis or fix the site of a country's capital. No, and the explanation is that Madrid is as much a city by royal decree as Petrograd, the result of Peter the Great's desire for a window looking out toward Europe. But even he selected a site where a river makes a harbour on an arm of the sea. Madrid has no river, only a small stream, the Manzanares ; it is not even a site of great natural security, something which made Toledo an obvious capital for so many centuries. Madrid is an old town but a new city, as European cities go. At the beginning of the 16th century it had only 3000 inhabitants, so of course we shall find it lacking stained glass made during that productive century. In passing, we may note that always the governing race in Spain has desired a centrally located capital. First the Visigoths and then the Moors and last the Spaniards themselves chose Toledo for that reason, and it was centuries on centuries before its glory passed.

It was Philip II who finally decided upon Madrid, the geographical centre of Spain, as the royal abode and the *unica corte*, or sole royal court. It was not, however, until the beginning of the 18th century that Madrid really came into its own, and now, thanks to its being the hub of radiating railways, it is become a fine modern city with broad avenues, stately public buildings, excellent subways, and other up-to-date conveniences of life, not the least important of which are several first-class hotels.

One feature of Madrid life seems strange to Americans, and that is the dinner hour,—all the world dines at nine o'clock or later. At first you fancy this a local exaggeration imposed by the fashionable world that always surrounds a court, but not so,—it is the custom of the country. At Sigüenza, still lacking a modern hotel, the modest posada near the railway station required the author to wait until 9.15 p.m. for dinner, but when it came it was worth waiting for, and its well-cooked courses amply repaid the delay.

The traveller must likewise accommodate himself to another local custom, that of shutting the shops during the early afternoon for the siesta that always follows luncheon. None reopen for business until 4.30, and many not until five, but when the city resumes business, there is an air of refreshed gaiety abroad.

We come to Madrid because it affords so excellent a centre for our trips.

Although it lacks ancient architectural embellishments, and of course old glass, the pictures of the Prado Museum and the display at the Royal Armoury are, to say the least, noteworthy substitutes. Not only does the Prado possess many and fine examples of all the European schools of painting, but also you will never really know Velasquez, that master-painter, until you stand before his great canvasses there. This experience is worth walking all the way from Paris to Madrid.

Of course you will go to a bull-fight. Whether or not you go to more than one is open to question !

Before saying more of this national institution,
just a word about its recent rival in Spain, football.
Interest in that man-building game has spread all
over the country like wild-fire ; everywhere they
are playing it, and everywhere crowds are flocking
to applaud the players. Their game, the English
Association, familiarly known as " soccer," is better
suited for a national sport than is our American
football, because our game, with its intricate plays
and memorized code of signals is too elaborate for
any and everybody to play. It is an inspiring
spectacle to see 78,000 people in the Yale Bowl
watching 22 players in their highly scientific
struggle, but soccer, like our baseball, can be played
anywhere by teams of individuals who do not have
to learn a lot of special plays or the signals to
operate them. The most sporting district of Spain
is Catalonia. It bears so high a continental
reputation in this regard that in 1922 at Paris its
athletic association was awarded the silver cup for
greatest progress during the year by the International Olympic Athletic Committee, on which
the author has the honour of representing the
United States. A Spanish friend reports that
public interest in football has recently become so

great it is now difficult to find level spaces enough to accommodate all the wouldbe players, and that attendance at their matches is hurting the bull-fights.

And now what shall we say of bull-fights? Picturesque in the extreme, yes, and theatrically appealing. But be careful not to ponder upon the aged horses, trampling on their own intestines gored out by the bulls. Sympathize even less with the bull thrust out into the glaring ring to be killed, but only after he has been systematically worn out by chasing red capes in every direction, by numerous banderillas thrust into him and by much goring of horses to tire his neck so that his drooping head will facilitate the final thrust of the matador's espada. Forget all this, and as much as possible fix your mind on the play of colour, the interweaving of gaily dressed figures, and the excited onlookers, learned in every detail of tiring and killing the bull, and vocal in the extreme. The picturesque veneer of this unfair contest is elaborate and well sustained. A real bull-fight would be glorious, that is, a bout between a fresh swordsman and a fresh bull, such as was customary in the Coliseum of ancient Rome. But long periods of bull-baiting and fatiguing, ending in jabbing the exhausted animal—well, the sooner the rising tide of Spanish football submerges this survival of one-sided mediæval brutality, the better for the youth and manhood of Spain ! Three cheers for their man-to-man football battles !—but decent interment for this outgrown, unfair theatrical display which, hard as it is on disembowelled horses and jaded bulls, is really worse for the spectators.

Zuloaga the great painter, himself a Spaniard, felt so strongly on this subject that he painted a picture showing a picador on the worst broken-down old white horse he could find. And now when an aged blindfolded white horse is led out into a Spanish bullring, a shudder will run round as the onlookers mutter " Zuloaga's horse." He affirmed that the picture could not be safely exhibited in such a bull-fighting centre as Seville, so bitter was the feeling it aroused among partisans of the game.

An outstanding leader in Spain's Renaissance of competitive sports is that hard-hitting polo-player and dashing motorist the King. During the summer of 1922, playing at Deauville as the Duke of Toledo, he materially aided the Madrid Polo

Team to win three sets of challenge cups. He
has a cross stroke with the mallet under his pony's
belly that is both unusual and effective, especially
in scrimmages along the side boards.

We shall visit Madrid to use it as a centre for
stained glass tours about the middle of Spain.
From here it will be convenient to run out by
motor or train to Segovia, Avila, Toledo, or the
Escorial, and by train to Sigüenza. Segovia and
Avila may be combined into the same day, either
by making the whole loop in a motor, or else by
going to Segovia by the morning train (three hours),
then on by motor 80 kilometres after luncheon to
Avila on another railroad line, and thence back to
Madrid, three hours by train. Or else Avila and
the Escorial can be similarly combined, for the
Escorial lies on the same railroad about an hour
from Madrid on the line to Avila. The roads
about Madrid are all practicable for motors, so
perhaps our tourist will prefer that method of
travel, especially as it means independence of
railway timetables. You start when you like,
stay as long as you choose, and turn back as soon
as your sightseeing is completed. Toledo is 70
kilometres from Madrid, two hours by rail, and there

is an excellent hotel at which to lunch. Sigüenza is two hours by express trains from Madrid on the line to Saragossa and Barcelona, but only the ultra-enthusiast will stop there, since the glass in not stained because of Cistercian regulations (see page 5).

SEGOVIA

AN ancient galleon of wide and ponderous bulk, lofty at bow and stern, and tugging at a single mooring, — such is Segovia, jutting out over the plain below, the great cathedral rising at her prow, and at the stern the Alcázar built by Romans upon Iberian foundations. The single tie between the high-perched city and the upland behind from which she is already cut off and seems ready to desert, is the thousand-foot long aqueduct over whose triple tier of slender arches the Romans fetched water for the city's need. Complete, apart, and serenely high this Segovia, full of crooked narrow streets disclosing quaint vistas, each a framed picture out of the past, its stately homes where dwelt grandees of old, all spelling the witchcraft of that potent witch, History. Its proud citizens will tell you that the cathedral is almost modern ; it was built, forsooth ! so late as 1577. Nevertheless, with all their ancestral pride in the city's hoary age, they welcome

73

to her Hall of Fame that distinguished modern Daniel Zuloaga who, installed in what was once the church of San Juan, has there painted such wonderful counterfeits of Spanish types against Spanish backgrounds. He and his contemporary, Sorolla, make a pair of whom Spain is justly proud, and their paintings are prized by collectors the world around.

There are two Spains, one gay, sunlit, almost playful—the other austere, brooding, darkly thoughtful. The former appeals to Sorolla, and with it he disports on land or in the ocean surf. Almost one fears to be splashed if standing too near a seaside picture of his ! But it is the sterner phase of Spanish life which inspires Zuloaga, and how faithfully he interprets it ! Whether it be men he paints or women, or even unpeopled landscapes, all is alive and eloquent of that Spain which drove out the Moor, which supported the Inquisition, which gloats over mangled horses at bull-fights, and above all passionately loves the rugged landscape of Spain. Somehow, to a foreigner it seems a distortion of Fate that it should be Zuloaga who was installed at Segovia. Zuloaga might better have dwelt at sterner Avila, and left the bright and cheerfully airy Segovia to Sorolla, wielder of the rainbow and splashing water.

The brightest spot in all Segovia, so bright that one welcomes its shady arcades, is the Plaza de la Constitucion, across one side of which stretches the great Cathedral, toward which our steps are bent. Entering by the north transept, directly from the glare of the sun outside, we find ourselves within the most pleasingly lighted church in Spain. To this impression of refreshment several factors contribute. First and foremost is the brilliancy of colouring which persists all round the row above row of ancient windows, whose total surpasses even that of Seville, for here are no less than 97. Another factor is that the lighting is almost entirely from above, and high up at that, while that which comes from below is purposely meagre. The chapels of the apse ambulatory have but one small embrasure each, mostly glazed in white. To these useful factors must be added a third, and one contributing materially to Segovia's charm,—the warm tone of the pinkish-brown stone, blushing with reflected colour from above, and harmonizing as it reflects. There is no church in Europe which can better be recommended to those wishing to learn how stained glass can beautify an interior by tempering without dulling the light.

The church has no real triforium, but instead there runs around the interior far above you a double row of clerestory lights. Almost all have three lancets, the central one taller than its companions : the upper row are but of one lancet each, and are only half the size of those in the tier below them. The arches at the top of these lancets seem almost round, so slightly are they pointed. In fact, it is not by much that they escape the charge of being dumpy. But what colour in all this top lighting ! —such deep reds and strong blues, and yellows which, in the apse, deeper than their fellows in the nave, border upon the orange.

Fortunately, it is at exactly the right point that we enter upon all this mellow glow. Before us open out the ample transepts, and high above the crossing rises the cimborio, a central lantern for all this tinted light. There are small windows on all four sides of the cimborio, but only those to the east and west are coloured. The waves of colour surging around the cathedral's interior so monopolize our capacity for enjoyment as fortunately to distract us from the drawing, which is poor. The glass here is almost all of the second half of the 16th century.

The treatment of the western façade is somewhat unexpected. There are none of the usual round embrasures, and the three windows, of unusually modest dimensions, are not divided into lancets. The central one, higher up, is glazed in white, while the two which flank it lower down on either side, one just above each small portal, are coloured in the late 16th century manner so uniformly observed all round this church. The nave is unusually rich in possessing 62 windows in colour, well worth careful inspection. Note the effective blue lettering in the second embrasure from the west, north side of the lower row. It is dated 1544, and makes one wish that more frequent use had been made of so highly decorative a motif. On this side of the nave all the glass is in good condition, but that across on the south side has sustained considerable damage. The records tell us that when in the 17th century repairing became necessary, a workshop was set up inside the church so that none of the old glass need be taken away. This was fortunate, because it resulted in repairs being effected with ancient fragments, so that harmonious colour effect was not disturbed nor diluted by the intermingling of later glass. Incidentally, we have here a proof (if proof be needed !) that while good colour is vital for successful effect, design is but secondary. For example, all the southerly windows are pleasing and contemporaneous, and yet the only well-preserved design is in the eastmost of the lower row. The old designs are gone, but the old colour still pleases. This latter window contains a good deal of red throughout its simulated architecture, a distinctly Spanish touch. The most interesting windows here are the two impressive redondas, one high up in the end of the north transept, and the other facing it in the south. The colour of both is completely satisfying, and needs no comment except that more green appears in the northern than in the southern. But the stone traceries in these large circular lights give us food for thought. The whole space of each is divided into four equal parts by a horizontal mullion crossing a perpendicular one, at their intersection cunningly intertwined and pierced for sundry small coloured panes serving to lighten the heavy stone mullions. What interests us is that these mullions are carved to simulate ribbons, a treatment

SEGOVIA CATHEDRAL
Its 97 windows were all glazed late in 16th century

so popular in the lettering both of the Visigoths and early Mexican tribes. Why is this fashion found at places so remote from each other and separated by the Atlantic Ocean ? Can it be that the masonry of these two Segovia redondas throws light on a problem so fully discussed in Ignatius Donnelly's " Lost Atlantis " ? He would have us believe that upon the island of Atlantis, long since submerged in mid-Atlantic, there originated an early civilization which, while it spread to Yucatan and Central America to the west, also penetrated so far to the east as Egypt. Can the intertwined ribbons on these Segovia windows be cousins of the ancient Maya ribbon decorations alongside the Caribbean Sea ? We know that Mayas communicated with distant friends through messages expressed in knotted ropes ;—do the intricate intertwinings of these Segovia mullions hide some mediæval message ? Quien sabe ?— as the Spaniard loves to say.

From Segovia to Avila is 80 kilometres, over a good road, and automobiles may be hired in either city.

AVILA

ALBRECHT DÜRER drew, and many romance readers have pictured for themselves, certain mediæval fortress cities stationed aloft in secure isolation and girt about by stern forbidding battlements, self-sufficient, disdainful ! Such another is Avila, its stout walls reinforced by over eighty sturdy towers all frowning down upon the dominated landscape. Perhaps there is elsewhere in Europe a more impressive picture from out the Middle Ages, but it is doubtful. Avila is more convincing than the too thoroughly restored Carcasonne, more picturesque than Aigues-Mortes, more martial than Orvieto. It is as if the pages of history had been turned back, and as you gaze upward upon its strength and beauty almost one expects a blare of trumpets to announce a group of armoured knights issuing forth from one of the narrow city gates.

But let us mount the winding road and, entering

the city, make our way to the Cathedral. To us under this ancient spell of old-world romance it seems but appropriate and natural that one of the bastions of those sturdy walls is afforded by the Cathedral's apse protruding eastward. This is as much as to say that every factor of the city's life, even its religion's Holy of Holies, must take its part in the common defence.

And once inside the Cathedral, the cold grey of its granite walls harshened by white lines of mortar, echo the austere note which this fortress city strikes. Especially to one freshly come from bright Segovia, where pinkish-brown walls so admirably reflect the Cathedral's glowing panes, is the sharpness of the contrast apparent. Particularly in the nave does one feel the stony harshness of wall and light, for here no coloured glass lends its tempering warmth. To be sure, the great west window has along the bottom of its eight lancets some faintly tinted squares of 17th century manufacture, but they were meant to be level with the observer's eye and are hardly noticeable at their present elevation. That we casual visitors are not the only ones to be chilled to the artistic marrow by the grey granite and the white mortar lines is proved by the fact that in the sacristy all these lines have been gilded.

The apse is not so glaringly lighted as the nave, for although all the lowest range of embrasures lack colour except the eastmost, there is much of it around the numerous clerestory and triforium lights, which by the way are of single lancets above and pairs below.

Avila glass reveals that it was made during a transition, not only from the 15th to the 16th centuries (for it was begun in 1497 by Juan de Santillana and Juan de Valdivieso) but also between the Gothic and the Classical or Renaissance periods. This is interestingly demonstrated around the apse, where the canopies on the north side are Renaissance in type, while those to the south are late Gothic. The principal contract for glazing was let in 1520 to Alberto de Hollanda, a Dutch glazier of Burgos, and it was given him by Bishop Francisco Ruiz, nephew of the great Cardinal Cisneros. Alberto was followed by his son, Nicolás de Hollanda.

But it is to the transepts that we must turn for the chief glories of Avila. The masonry of these two roomy wings mutely testifies that once they did not extend so boldly from the church as now, because

AVILA CATHEDRAL
Looking towards apse which, protruding, forms a bastion of the city walls

the inward half of their side walls differs materially from their outward portion. Not only is the light here softened by much and rich colour, but as further precaution against glare all the westerly embrasures of both transepts are blocked up. We shall see this latter device again when we visit Hoogstraeten, up in Belgium.

At the ends of both transepts are two tall windows, each with a pair of lancets, below tracery lights which in the south are of the usual trefoil or fourfoil type. At the north the pair of triangular lights above the lancets is capped by a small ojo, similar in size and treatment to those along the nave chapels in Bologna Cathedral.

We have noted that the side walls of the transepts record two building periods, and show just where and how they were extended. The newer or outward half of the easterly wall in both transepts has a large four-lancetted window with pierced traceries above, all glazed in the usual 16th century manner. But inward from this embrasure, still in the east wall of both transepts, we find a triumph of window making resembling nothing to be seen in Spain. Indeed, the only prototype anywhere is the broad window at Coventry, England, where a gallery of nine splendid kings stretches across the entire end of the principal room at the Guild Hall, all to the greater glory of Henry VII, proudly posted in the middle. Here at Avila, these two embrasures, much wider than they are high, contain to the south eight lancets, and the north six. As the arch swings in above these bundles of perpendicular lights, the space it encloses contains elaborate and pierced traceries. The northerly group of six lancets differs slightly from its companion of eight by culminating in a small ojo above the pointed arch. To prevent the southerly and wider one from looking too broad the architect has run up its centre a mullion that, at the top of the lancet, splits and swings right and left as in English embrasures of the Perpendicular period (15th century). Can it be that an Englishman had to do with this work? Certainly someone engaged here had at least seen how English taste was correcting the monotonous effect of too many perpendicular lines. Below this wide embrasure are set two others of two lancets each, so that altogether this easterly illumination more than offsets the blocking of the embrasures opposite along the transepts' west walls.

The glazing of these superb early windows

hints at a date later than do the stone frames, for the former is perfected Renaissance. Not only are the canopies of completely classical design, but also between them and each lancet-top are cherubs, garlands, and other dainty details then popular. This interpolation of decorative fancies above the canopies is a purely Spanish touch, but it conforms to the craze for elaboration of ornament demanded by the Renaissance spirit everywhere.

It is at the Cathedral that one chiefly senses the gloomy ghost of Torquemada, who brought death to so many compatriots, but his body lies in the Monastery of Santo Tomas, outside the walls and down the hill. Fortunately, Santo Tomas leaves other and more artistic memories, especially that of the charming alabaster tomb of young Prince John, only son of King Ferdinand and Queen Isabella. Here also are two small 16th century windows, one beside the altar and the other in the north end of the crossing. In San Vicente, just outside the city's south-west gate, the cimborio has two diminutive lights of the 16th century. There is a fine wheel-window in the west façade of San Pedro, just above the portal. That it is of an early period is proven by the columns that radiate from its centre. Notice that each column swerves slightly, lending the effect of revolving motion to the wheel—very interesting, whether intentional or not.

If one travels to and from Avila by train, he will miss its most picturesque effect unless willing to undertake a short excursion out through the Puerta del Puente and down below the walls on the opposite side from the railway station. Below the ramparts runs the river Adaja, and for one stationed on its bridge, or better still up the hill beyond, at a stone cross called Cruz de los Cuatro Postes, there is best seen this amazing picture snatched bodily out of the Middle Ages, a strong city belted round by bulwarks and towers, frowning down from its heights, Avila the oft beleaguered !

EARLY WHEEL WINDOW, SAN PEDRO, AVILA
Note that columns swerve slightly, lending appearance of rotation to wheel

TOLEDO

A TOLEDO blade never had a superior, and so it is but fitting that Toledo's warlike part in Spanish history should be a trenchant and a stirring tale. Once upon a time, a race of Arab Moslems from Africa invaded the Iberian peninsula, settled down and made it their home. During four long centuries one of their chiefest strongholds was Toledo. Its secure site, a flat-topped hill girdled by two rivers that had gashed ravines on all sides, has long attracted the notice of men trained to war. Nearly two centuries before Christ the Romans had wrested it from the Carpetani because they needed an outpost so defended by nature. Those virile conquerors the Visigoths recognized its strategic value by making it their capital. All this was long before the Spaniard, moving downward from the province of Asturias, rough cradle of his race, began the long struggle with the Moslems. It was not until 1085 that Alfonso VI of Castile, aided by the mighty

Cid Campeador, added Toledo to a Spain that was then only in the making. We are told that, as the Spanish outpost and capital, its population grew to the amazing total of 200,000, but though that seems an exaggeration for a walled enclosure now comfortably accommodating 20,000, Toledo was undoubtedly a city of signal importance. Commercially, too, it possessed great significance, for its wool trade and its incomparable weapons brought ever increasing wealth.

Much of Toledo's history is told in stone and brick. Many and widely differing are the chapters, beginning with early Roman and Visigothic remains and coming down through delightful synagogues of arabic architecture, the stately Cathedral, and that bijou of Gothic, San Juan de los Reyes, and ending far back of our time in the house and garden of the painter Greco now restored to the condition in which he saw it. And yet there is much more to be told of Toledo than its architecture records. The most truthful picture the author ever saw of this historic city was one painted by Zuloaga as background for a full length portrait of a Toledan grandee who, alertly erect, dominated the left foreground. So realistic was the harshness of its

88

rugged detail as to mark one's memory. Ever since Toledo has meant the builded city plus its citizens, life within its Spanish frame, dwellings rather than structures of stone. The list of Toledan attractions is far longer than either of the quaint bridges leading one over the rivers into its well-defended enceinte. And once inside it needs but a few hours to show why men have loved and fought for Toledo all down the ages. As a museum city, crowded with mediæval treasures, it excels even Nuremburg and Rouen.

Although the total of 77 ancient coloured windows in the Cathedral falls below that of Leon, Segovia, and Seville, nevertheless it impresses one as having even more than the two latter. Certainly nowhere else is such a high level of general excellence attained as here. The colour is uniformly of a delightful richness—even the canopy framing abandons its conventional yellow stain and greys to riot in deep tones that nowise yield in robustness to Italian glass at its ripest. Then, too, Toledo boasts of certain features unique in glazing, chief among which is its fashion of introducing large circles of contrasting colour as frames. This is seen along the nave walls between the clerestory and the chapel tops, and also across the west façade, below the rose window. These circular frames done in narrow lines of green, red, blue, or mauve enclose Biblical scenes, and are generally careless of mullions, for nearly always they swing across two lancets. Sometimes, when there are six lancets, the circular frame spanning the two central ones will be poised higher than its companions uniting the side pairs. This design contributes materially to a balance of composition. It is interesting that only at Toledo did men of a later period thus emulate 13th century glaziers, whose medallions likewise grouped pictures in a fashion decorative as well as orderly. At Toledo the ancient idea has its reincarnation with a broader swing and greater freedom of scope (see frontispiece).

Then again the Toledo artists disregarded another widely accepted convention by treating in a style all their own the saint-within-canopy tradition so scrupulously respected all over Europe. Only in Spain, but best and more frequently at Toledo, is the space above the saint's head within the canopy, filled with Renaissance details such as garlands, cherubic heads, etc.

The books like to say that the glazing at Toledo

TOLEDO CATHEDRAL.   NAVE
Early 15th century : a stately series running along both sides of nave.   Note graceful
treatment of tracery lights above grouped lancets

begins with 1418, and that the earliest it possesses is along the nave. Perhaps they are right, but only if they mean glass expressly manufactured by contract for this Cathedral. If, however, there be no such reservation, then we must "respectfully dissent," for there is much clearly earlier than that date. For example, look up at the windows along the eastern sides of both transepts. The brassy yellow bits, separately leaded in where needed, obviously antedate the discovery of yellow stain early in the 14th century, and are therefore nearly a hundred years older than their rivals in the nave. It is only fair to add (and this endorses the reservation just suggested) that these transept panes were doubtless transported hither from narrower and earlier embrasures either of this church or some other. A well-known case of this same sort of thing is seen in Exeter Cathedral, where 14th century glass fills 15th century stone framework, and, alas ! is cut to fit it, like the unfortunate occupants of Procrustes' bed. It is fortunate that in the Toledo transepts the ancient panes did not need to be cut down. On the contrary, they were not quite large enough for their new quarters, so were eked out on each side with later glass. We suggest that two of these windows, those furthest from the centre on each side of the apse opening, are slightly older than their mates. The brilliant deep reds and blues of this pair have been delighting observers ever since early in the 14th century. And even earlier, surely of late 13th century, is the glazing of the north rose.

Much later than these ancient four-lancetted transept lights are their splendid companions across on the westerly side of both transepts, with elaborately decorated traceries capping double galleries of eight lancets on the south, or seven on the north. Nor is this wealth of shimmering beauty all that those spoiled children the transepts can boast, for at their northerly and southerly ends high up are swung gorgeous rosetones, that to the north a real rose of primitive type, while fronting it to the south is a fully fledged petal window of sixteen splendid leaves. Note that this latter has green for background within its leaves, while the older one has blue in the circular openings composing it, except at the centre, which is red. Both these treatments follow the best tradition of their respective periods. In the older, the circle at the hub shows the Crucifixion, the six closest around it St. Mary, St. John, and four angels, and in the twelve outer circles are the twelve greater prophets, pointing towards Christ on His Cross at the centre.

The apse glazing yields but grudgingly to the transepts' claim of supremacy, its 25 coloured lights gloriously illuminating this crowning feature of the Cathedral, toward which all the rest of the interior leads up. Its clerestory has at the west groups of four lancets, of which the side ones are shorter than the two central, above which latter gracefully poise small ojos. The two eastmost lights have but three lancets, the central one taller than its mates.

The apse ambulatory has a pierced triforium and, above it, four lights on each side, half of which are filled with coloured pierced traceries, while the other half has each an ojo held in place by the points of the surrounding cusps. The choir chapels are also rich in early colour.

Turning from the extreme eastern end of the vast Cathedral we espy far off at the western extremity its magnificent rose window guarded below by a superb battalion of five double-lancetted lights. Along this gallery is exhibited the same Toledan treatment as above the nave chapels, viz. circles in

93

colour, each swinging across a pair of lights with refreshing disregard for stout stone mullions. What care they for mere stone ?—is not colour more alive than it ?—and do they not carry the eye along with them so as almost to make us forget the mullions ? They most certainly do, so that the success of their compulsion completely justifies their existence.

This 15th century rose (1418-25) is more concentric, and less radiating, has smaller and more numerous elements than it would had it been of the 14th century. Up within the central ojo of the roseton there is displayed upon a faint yellow ground not the customary figure, but instead, the red hat and pendant tasselled fringe of the Cathedral's presiding prelate. Around about it are disposed no less than seven circuits of differently shaped panes, one outside another, an opulence of glazing that is brilliantly effective. Note that when one is studying the exterior of this façade there is no hint of this roseton, for it is hidden by the narthex rising in front of it. Strangely enough, when this window is viewed from the inside, one does not notice that back of all its splendid glass rises so ponderous a structure as the narthex.

TOLEDO CATHEDRAL.   WEST ROSETON

Constructed 1418-25.   The Spanish Rose at its acme of blossoming.   Below runs gallery
of five pairs of lancets, each pair united by a coloured circular frame shown in frontispiece.

Down at the left corner of the west façade is the Mozarabic chapel, with two small lights glazed in the usual 16th century manner by Juan de la Cuesta, who also repaired many of their earlier neighbours. This chapel is rather an awkward reminder for us Christians that during the four centuries of Moslem occupation the practice of Christian rites was permitted here, but that when Christianity won the city it showed no such toleration for the faith of Islam !

And now for the side walls of the nave, which are divided horizontally into three courses—the chapels below, the lights along the wall of the nave aisles above the chapels, and then, highest of all, the clerestory. Along the south side there are four chapels with windows containing saints within late Gothic canopies. All the north side chapels have white panes but one, which is necessary, because the roof of the cloister walk outside cuts off so much light. Along the south side of the nave, running above the chapels, are six large embrasures, and to the north five, all handsome, well balanced, and ample, and all displaying the coloured circles already described, so unique a motif in this craft. The episodes within the

morning, have the whole day there until six in the
evening, when the express will take him to Leon,
arriving at 11 p.m. From Leon he may take a
local train running out to Astorga in an hour and
a quarter, and either return thence directly to
Madrid, or via Leon.

TOLEDO CATHEDRAL
Roseton above Puerta del Reloj (Gate of the Clock). Note well balanced adjustment
of roseton to the wall, general in Spain

ASTORGA

AFTER sundry final puffs and grunts of the engine, the train slowly comes to a stop in the station. It is 5 a.m. on a dark night, with only a few stars to relieve the silent blackness of the sky. Sleepily we tumble out of the comfortable sleeping-car on to an almost deserted platform. Why the mischief didn't I go straight through Leon to Oviedo and pick up Astorga on the way back ! A half-dozen yawning fellow-passengers seem equally regretful of their arrival, and cigarettes begin to twinkle their ineffectual lights. I alone of all the company seem uninformed upon the momentous question of how to get to the hotel,—any hotel ! The rest slowly head for the Salida, where tickets are shown to a somnolent railway official whose subconscious self (apologies to Coué !) seems competent through experience to punch the cardboard slips without awakening him. Out we all file into the formless night and climb dreamily into what, in its youth, used to be an omnibus. We are only six, but we pack it tight. Inside the darkness is even blacker than without ; so low is the visibility that nothing exists but cigarette ends. There comes a gruesome feeling born of reading Gautier's "Voyage en Espagne" that perhaps these men are bandits !— or that possibly our insect powder ought to be in our pocket instead of in the bag, especially as the said bag is now remote, piled upon the bus's top. Soon both anxieties pass—Daniel is not in the lions' den,—there are no insects, and besides, the possible banditti prove harmless commercial travellers, as their self-starting talk rapidly develops. In passing, it is fair to comment that travel in Spain is much freer from the pest of insects than in Italy or southern France. The traveller next us announces that he has been to Chicago and that he speaks English. Inside two minutes he proves the former statement and disproves the latter. All this while the ancient vehicle is lumbering up an incline through the Stygian darkness. Presently it halts, voices are heard, we have arrived, and climbing down into the dim starlight confront a blinking housemaid standing at a door in the glare of one small oil lamp. A board with painted numbers is against the wall as we enter, and keys hang under the numbers. Inquiries from the reformed banditti reveal which rooms are occupied and which not, whereupon they allot among themselves those known from previous visits to be worthy of choice. My near-Chicago acquaintance proffers me his advice on this important point, but now in the Spanish tongue, for his English has given out, or perhaps it only functions by daylight, or else does not keep well in this climate. Up the dark stairs, armed with a key and a candle apiece, marches our yawning column. Soon each of us is catching a beauty sleep until daylight shall have come.

Such is the manner of our arrival at Astorga. Do not do likewise, for we advise you to run out here, an hour and a quarter by train from Leon, on your way from Madrid either to or from Oviedo. Astorga by daylight will prove but little less sleepy than it was before dawn. The Cathedral alone will excite interest, and its twenty-nine windows of the early 16th century repay your visit. Its choir stalls, too, are fine and in excellent preservation. The windows here are very unequal in their excellence, unusually so for Spain, where generally that which a church possesses is almost altogether excellent, good, or passable. At Astorga the colour, however, is generally satisfactory, no matter what may be alleged against the drawing, and it is more important under Spanish skies for the colouring to be sufficiently strong than it is for the design to be of marked excellence.

The best glass is in the grouping of two double-lancetted embrasures belonging to the chapel at the south-east corner, between the apse and the south side portal. Here are gorgeous reds, faded blues, and vegetable greens, along with much powerful yellow and brown in the simulated stone-work. Across the left-hand pair of lancets is spread a Nativity, and across the right hand, a Circum-cision. Hovering over the former are angels against blue, while above the latter note the pleasant use of sage green in the curtains of the brown balde-quin rising over the officiating High Priest. This soft green is reminiscent of Italy, where it was a favourite tint of many glaziers. The side lights of this cosy chapel show a double tier of single figures under Renaissance canopies. This same type of saints within similar niches runs in a double tier all around the six apse windows (each of three lancets), and are also in those lights which at the east end flank the apse.

On the south side of the nave the chapels are low, only half as high as those on the north. This means that the south chapels have only room for very small embrasures, about one foot by two in dimensions, but on the north side the chapels have ample windows, generally of four lancets with coloured tracery lights above. In the fifth of these latter chapels from the west, the artist has divided his space in two by a horizontal gallery painted across it. Above are the dainty details of cherubs, etc., so dear to the Spanish Renaissance, while the lower half is given over to an Adoration of the Magi, who face the Virgin seated on the right.

Up along the south wall of the nave, and above the low chapels, are large windows, of which we shall prefer the fourth from the west, once more a Circumcision scene, but this time on a larger scale. Its drawing is not so satisfactory as its colour, which is strong and well sustained. Even the marbles that construct the Temple across its four lancets are of brilliant hues, and remind one of Italy's pre-eminence in this regard. Indeed, these gaily tinted marbles and the sage green in the other

103

Circumcision down in the south-east chapel give grounds for suspecting either a " fine Italian hand " among the glaziers here, or else that one or more of them had visited Arezzo or Florence.

Next this window to the east is one filled with the single saints in Renaissance canopies so popular throughout this church. The central pair of the four lancets has each a two-storied canopy. Of the ojo de buey here, one can only say that it has a 17th century green and magenta boss at the centre.

A cleaning and restoration of the interior walls has recently taken place, and is being supplemented by a relaying of the worn pavement. All this renovation is being carried out in a better taste than is shown in the ultra-modernity of the new Episcopal Palace hard by, which must be seen to be believed !

OVIEDO

UP in the north-west corner of Spain lie the provinces of Asturias and Galicia, peopled with a numerous and worthy type of Spaniard. In fact, perhaps thanks to their equable climate, those two districts are so densely populated that large numbers emigrate yearly to Argentina, which heartily welcomes such industrious additions to its citizenship. Every year there land at Buenos Ayres about 250,000 emigrants, half from north-western Spain and half from northern Italy. No country receives a better class of emigrant. During the author's service there as American Minister, he studied this useful stream of new citizens and conceived a high opinion of them. Of late years the Spanish government has taken steps to keep these migrating Galicians and Asturians at home by initiating public works such as roads, etc., to provide better paid employment.

The historical importance of Asturias as the

cradle of the Spanish race, the starting place for their slow but steady acquisition of the whole peninsula, is well known. It is officially recorded in the fact that ever since 1388 the heir to the Spanish throne has borne the title of Prince of the Asturias. Furthermore, these two north-westerly districts contain Spain's principal natural wealth, for there are located most of her valuable iron, lead, and coal deposits. Mountainous as are these provinces, there is much fertile and highly cultivated land in their valleys, and excellent harbours along their coasts.

The capital of Asturias is Oviedo. The admirably placed Gothic cathedral, its beauty enhanced by a lofty Renaissance tower, contains fine 15th century glass. Even the unenthusiastic Baedeker is moved to announce that " the tracery and stained glass of its spacious windows make a noble and harmonious impression." Especially fine are those in the Capilla Mayor, which is located in the five-sided apse with an ambulatory running around it. In the clerestory here are five great three-lancetted windows, all handsomely glazed, and lower down seven more, but against two of the latter rise the great retablo of five sections dating from the 15th and 16th centuries. Each bay of the nave has a flamboyant six-lancetted window. Along the south side they contain 15th century glass, but opposite, on the north, the embrasures are blocked up.

LEON

" A Castilla y a Leon
Nuevo mundo dió Colon "

SO sang a Spaniard who came after Columbus, for the great navigator himself died without knowing it was a new hemisphere he had discovered. He thought it but an outlying portion of the island of Zipangu (Japan), whose fabulous riches Marco Polo had reported upon his return to Europe in 1292. The fact was, Columbus thought he had found a short route to Japan,—nothing more, nothing less. He did not discover America,—others discovered that he had discovered America. Speaking of Marco Polo, it is curious how Italy seems always to have possessed the same property as radium—the ability to throw out bits without impoverishing herself,—a Marco Polo serving for twenty years as Chinese Viceroy of a Chinese province,—a Christopher Columbus to discover as a Spaniard a new hemisphere to enrich geography, but first to enrich Spain.

The couplet with which we began does not name Spain as the gainer by his amazing enterprise—it says Castile and Leon, but this meant the Spain of those days. True, the Spaniards had already developed southwards from the cradle of the race in the rugged province of Asturias. The new possessions in the interior had been consolidated, Castile in the centre adjoining Leon on the west. The long struggle with the Moslem holders of the peninsula's southern half was then approaching a climax, for victorious Castile and Leon were rolling ponderously southward, but not yet were they Spain. 1492 marks not only the date of Columbus' gift of the new world to Castile and Leon, but also it heralds the final wresting from the Moors of the government of Granada.

This Leon, then, that we are visiting for a draught from the sparkling fount of beauty which is its glass, is not merely a city or province of Spain—we are back again in the days when with its neighbour Castile it *is* the Spain of a glorious epoch in the Middle Ages. Then it was the heart of Spain, not merely one of many members, and therefore the pulsing waves of colour echoing up and down Leon Cathedral afford a sure way of attuning ourselves to the heart-beats of those spacious days. Leon is a colourful epic out of Spain's glorious past. Just as waves of sound carry messages, so shall the waves of tinted light here enable us to sense the taste, the feeling, the artistic perceptions of a race of men who, if they lacked the achievements of modern science, surely have no rivals in the field of modern glass.

Leon has little to offer the tourist outside its cathedral walls. The Casa de los Guzmanes built by Bishop Quiñones, the Colegiata de San Isidoro,— yes, interesting and fine, but many Spanish cities possess prototypes equally excellent. It is the glass of the cathedral that brings one here, rejoices him who sees it with a new and lasting joy, and then sends him away with a deeply graven memory that risks no obliteration at the hands of time. It is one of the great sights of Europe.

Spain is perhaps the most fortunate of all European countries in the manner of the restoration of her ancient monuments, and the most intelligently artistic of all her restorations is that to which this cathedral was subjected.

It is a favourite fancy for poets to speak of bowers of light, but where is there such another

LEON CATHEDRAL.   NORTH SIDE OF NAVE

Shows great size of these windows, their four anciently glazed lancets flanked by single narrow ones, formerly blocked
up but re-opened and re-glazed in modern times, as were also the triforium series seen running along below

as this ! The famous Chartres Cathedral shows a more serious turn of mind in its " dim, religious light " due to many lead lines and the less translucent glass of an earlier period. At the other end of the gamut of lighting are Sées Cathedral, and St. Ouen at Rouen, showing that revulsion against insufficient illumination which the 14th century demanded in France. *Chefs d'œuvres* of glazed chapels such as at King's College, Cambridge, or the Sainte Chapelle in Paris, are too small to be compared to the ampler glories of Leon. And so it goes, all through the list of churches completely glazed in colour and of no matter which country,— Leon always keeps the lead ! Perhaps its only serious competitor is Le Mans Cathedral, but even that impressive interior must take second place.

Every one of the many Leon Cathedral windows is glazed in colour. Perhaps they are even too numerous and ample for so sunny a land,—for clearly here is a cathedral copied from a northern type. But the effect is so magnificently luminous as to beat down any criticism. And in what manner shall we approach the delight which awaits any one entering the portals of Leon Cathedral ?

Shall it be in orderly fashion, or shall we follow the example of the colour running riot all about us and cast order to the winds ?   Why not let impulse be our guide ?   Even though the reader be of orderly mind, and inclined by disposition to proceed deliberately to a reasoned examination of the panes, nevertheless we advise him for once to accept the Abbot of Unreason as a guide.   Consent to stroll aimlessly about this sanctuary whose light and colour is nowhere surpassed.

"To walk into Leon Cathedral is my idea of walking into the glory of God," writes a valued correspondent, and how could his description be improved upon !   The letter came from an officer of a National Bank in one of our far western states, so its expression is not that of a professional artist or literary man, and therefore may be taken as fairly recording how the average American will be affected by the Leon glass.   Here is what the French call a " cri de cœur " ; and that it comes straight from the American heart, you will understand when you visit the spot yourself.

Wander about, then, to your heart's content and soak your soul with brilliant contentment.

When the moment comes for more orderly

study then we must confess it is foolhardy to suggest a single viewpoint from which to obtain the best effect—there are so many such. One hint, however, will surely be useful because showing something seen in no other cathedral. The choir here, as usual in Spain, is installed in the nave, running two bays westerly from the crossing of the transepts. It consists of the usual choir-stalls backed by a high partition, but at Leon these stalls and their protecting partitions are interrupted in the middle of their western side, the space being filled in by a large sheet of plain glass permitting a view through to the High Altar, far off in the apse. When the afternoon sun comes through the west rose-window a reflection of its pattern is cast upon this glass partition. By standing a few paces west of the screen and facing east, you can so adjust this reflected image of the western rose that it fits just above the mass of kindred colour to the east in a manner most joyful. In a word, you may enjoy the eastern and western display at the same time, thus assembled for your benefit with no effort on your part. Could anything be more obliging !

It is interesting to note that although all the windows of the amply lighted triforium and also

all below it are modern, nevertheless it is but fair
to admit that this newer glazing does not sing out
of tune with the glorious older notes ringing out
above. Along the lowest range of embrasures the
modern designs are quite simple, twining vines,
etc., whilst heraldic blazons in colour upon grisaille
run all around the triforium gallery. In repairing
the old glass as well as supplying the new, the Chapter
was fortunate in having the co-operation of Juan
Bautista Lázaro, now deceased. He made careful
water-colour drawings of all the ancient glass that
remained, showing its condition at the time the
repairs were begun, which bits were missing, etc.
The author had the privilege of studying these
drawings in the home of that distinguished
Spanish architect, Lamperez y Romea, to whom
the Chapter had lent them. Lázaro discovered
during his researches that sometimes the mediæval
glazier, instead of colouring his glass design for a
window, put letters or numbers upon its parts
to indicate which hue of glass must be cut to fill
that special place. For example, on the ancient
Leon cartoons X meant red, L blue, V yellow, etc.
The greater or less intensity of each tone was shown
by adding Roman numerals in front or behind,

LEON.   WEST ROSETON
Flamboyant effect fully developed

e.g. LI meant the strongest blue, while IX a light red, or, in other words, pink.

It was probably Lázaro's artistic spirit which conceived the sympathetic idea that since the upper zone of the Leon windows (clerestory, etc.) was devoted to subjects celestial (saints, etc.), the second or triforium zone should be given over to matters worldly represented by royal, episcopal, and noble coats of arms, whilst the lowest range of windows should be of the earth earthy, and must therefore show vines and other growing things that spring from the ground.

Some idea of Leon's great wealth of coloured panes is given by saying that they cover no less than 1800 square metres, distributed over 737 panels or 230 windows, many of them forty feet high.

The most interesting window in the whole church is undoubtedly the large one, fifth from the west in the north clerestory of the nave. Indeed, it is among the three or four most interesting in Europe. Its subject is unique, since it portrays a series of episodes taken from the secular civil life of the Middle Ages, instead of following the almost invariable custom of showing religious subjects. Its panels were transferred hither from

a destroyed royal palace in Leon. This huge
embrasure is so far above the ground, and its late
13th or early 14th century figures so diminutive
that it needs to be studied with the aid of an opera
or field glass. Stand against the south wall of the
nave between the second and third bays from the
west. You will find yourself inspecting a cross-
section of Sport as known and practised during the
Middle Ages. The scenes unfold one above
another, six in each of the three lancets, the fourth
being devoted to more erudite matters such as
figures representing Rhetoric, etc. Eleven horsemen, depicting the king, queen, nobles, etc., prance
across the panes intent on such popular sports
as hunting, and their brown, red, white, and bay
horses are very diverting. So, too, is the camel
in the lower left-hand corner, to say nothing of
the elephant and the monkeys, all showing that
mediæval Spaniards declined to be stay-at-homes.
These secular episodes are not all sporting in
character, for some of the figures are writing books,
painting miniatures, etc. This window fills us
with a deep regret that there has survived so meagre
an amount of secular glass-painting as compared
with the quantities of the religious type. It is

obvious, however, that the strife so prevalent all through the Middle Ages did not imperil the glazing of religious houses so much as it did the homes of the devotees of Mars.

The remaining early glass of the church is collected into the westmost embrasure of the southerly nave clerestory, next the clock-tower, and also in the first, second, and fourth chapels of the apse. All this is surely of the 13th century. From those early days down through every period into the 18th century the great church steadily continued enriching itself with the best type of contemporary glazing.

For sheer limpidity of colouring, done in spelndid pot-metal reds and blues Spain has nothing to compare for mass effect with the two tiers of huge 14th century figures stationed all around the clerestory of the apse except in its eastmost light, where five cartouches rise one above the other within garish modern borders of red and yellow. But this modern indiscretion is forgiven because one cannot take one's eyes off these stately folk

> "High up like misty warders, dimly seen
> Moving at morn on some Burgundian wall."

Mere size is seldom a recommendation, but here it

certainly is, lending importance and dignity to these archaic personages standing guard above and about the High Altar. Positively stunning is the bold sweep of red, blue, and white masses that paint their garments. Very effective, too, is the large lettering here introduced, as are also a couple of pale green haloes with golden rims noticeable in the upper tier.

The chapels around the apse contain, in addition to the 13th century panes already mentioned, many fine examples of later date and especially of the 16th century. The three most easterly windows have two lancets each, and although they follow the curve of the apse, nevertheless the story of the Nativity swings across all six lancets. Such frank disregard not only of mullions but also of intervening wall space does not elsewhere exist. In the central pair of lancets is Jesus in the manger, and the Virgin Mary. The pair to the left show the adoring shepherds, while that on the right (bearing date 1565) has the Magi riding up through the woods bearing golden vessels and other gifts in their hands, and above them the Star of Bethlehem. Very pleasing is the use of varying tints of green in the foliage, all in agreeable contrast to

LEON CATHEDRAL.   APSE
Early 14th century.   Most ancient glass ensemble in Spain.   The limpidity of primitive
colours, here used in masses, is unsurpassed anywhere

the golden and grandiose architecture of the central lancets.

The limpid reds and blues of pot-metal glass in the easterly clerestory of the apse are in marked contrast to the considerable use of early green in the westerly portion of this clerestory. This employment of green is carried round the corner into the north transept, but not into the southerly one. The glass along the easterly wall of both transepts is markedly earlier than that opposite in the westerly ones. This same difference is also to be seen in the Toledo transepts.

Along the easterly transept wall stand in two tiers gigantic single figures of archaic drawing ; the rich reds and blues used in the two windows to the south show they had a different maker from him who used so much green in the northerly pair. Across in the westerly wall of the transepts, the pair of embrasures to the north are like the southerly pair in showing three tiers, one above the other, of deeply hued figures ; furthermore, the general treatment of all four is similar.

And now for the gorgeous rosetones that fill the two ends of the transepts. The first thing that strikes the visitor is that, contrary to custom, the framework of both huge sixteen-petalled roses is alike. This is most unusual, but is explained by the fact that the south rose is a modern reconstruction, and copied after its neighbour across the transepts. But this is the only similarity, for the glass differs widely both in colour and design. The south rose gives a distinctly reddish impression, shows considerable repairing with modern glass, and is nothing like so pleasing as its twin sister opposite. In this latter, there is no one predominating colour. Its great petals contain red and blue strap-work instead of the modern grisaille used in the southern one, and it has dark or light blue backgrounds instead of the southerly one's red. Both roses are alike in having a seated figure in the central circle, small single figures in the outer sixteen ojos, and Renaissance details in the half circles forming the outer rim. Thanks to the admirable windows in the side walls and these " heavenly twins " of rosetones, the transepts are surpassingly delightful.

One mild criticism must, however, be permitted us lest we seem indiscriminately laudatory, and here it is—tucked away (fortunately !) in the lower west corner of the north transept is a rather dreadful window showing Santiago (St. James) appearing in the clouds to aid the Spaniards struggling below him with the Moors. You will surely sympathize with the disgusted expression on the face of a wounded Moor in the foreground. His prophetic eye must have foreseen this picture !

Along the clerestory of the nave, on each side, there run six lofty and broad windows all of four ample lancets plus a narrow one on each side. These narrow slits appear even around the apse. They were formerly all blocked up, which must have looked badly because it does not do to have some lancets glazed and adjoining ones not. During the restoration of the old glass, these narrower flanking lancets were reopened and glazed with modern colour, which unfortunately quarrels with the older material alongside.

High up along the south nave wall are three tiers of single figures, all strongly coloured and contrasting with the lighter tints opposite. We have already commented on the civil life or sports window, fifth from the west on the north side of the clerestory, and upon the early panels collected into the westmost on the south side.

The ample western wheel-window, twenty-five

feet across, is charming. The Virgin with the Infant Jesus is seated in the central compartment. They are encircled by the twelve Apostles filling the spokes of the wheel, all full length and upright, radiating from the centre like herrings packed in a barrel—an effect more logical than artistic. The two outer encircling lights are filled with decorative details in the usual Spanish manner.

It is more in the nave than elsewhere that one notices the modern glass along the triforium and especially below it. This is because there are here no chapels to obstruct the view. The flowing lines of the vines and plants composing the designs are inoffensive, and less obtrusive than modern glass is apt to be. Nevertheless, our advice is to elevate your glance if you wish your spirit of appreciation uplifted, for the softer patine taken on by old glass lends it more charm than modern material can hope to yield.

Once more back in Madrid from our invasion of the north-western provinces, we shall now set forth due south to Seville, again by a night's journey, the most comfortable one in Spain.

in Spain and Flanders

Tourists wishing to visit Cordova and its wonderful Moorish mosque (where there is no ancient glass) will have to leave the train at the unpleasant hour of 5 a.m., but we wise glass pilgrims will reach Seville at a comfortable time for breakfast.

SEVILLE

ONE of the finest portraits ever painted is that of Emperor Charles V by Titian which hangs in the Prado Museum. The proud conqueror is mounted on his war-charger, armed cap-à-pie in the gold bedight armour still to be seen in the Royal Armoury. The cold stern face is that of one possessing all and yet knowing its emptiness. This Charles V is well known to history, and seen of all men who pass by Madrid. This is the mighty emperor, incarnation of Spain at the height of her supremest power. But there was another Charles V. Come to Seville, pass the portal of the Alcázar Palace, press on to its charming gardens, penetrate one after another of their hedged enclosures, on past flowered parterres until at the very centre of all, we come upon a small open space where stands a graceful pavilion of dainty proportions—el pabellon de Carlos Quinto—a retreat into Nature's heart. He who retired hither is certainly not the armoured warrior-statesman of the Prado, nor is he the jaded and disillusioned man who, casting off all pomp of power, betook himself to end his days in preparation for the Last Trump at the monastery of Yuste. Every student of history knows both Charles V as painted by Titian, and also him who exchanged imperial robes for the monk's coarse cowl. Few travellers know, and nowhere but in this garden refuge can one meet this same Charles, still powerful and not yet disillusioned, withdrawn into the heart of Nature, secluded by that which grows from that which is built, yielding to that impulse surviving in every man's heart ever since his first ancestor was driven from the Garden of Eden. No one ever really comprehends this new facet of that strange character until he, seated where Charles used to sit, looks out as he did upon this enclave of nature with its orange blossoms, its bushes of rivalling foliage, the soft blue of the ancient tiled seats, and listens to the incessant gossip of the plashing fountains. To understand this strange side of the great conqueror yielding to the long inbred lure of a garden, there is needed an echo out of old Japan. In Kyoto are two delicious gardens, the Kin-kakuji or Golden Pavilion of the

14th century, and the 15th century Gin-kakuji or Silver Pavilion. To these pleasaunces withdrew respectively the two mighty Ashikaga Shoguns, Yoshimitsu and Yoshimasa, ostensibly to escape the myriad cares of public life, but really without relinquishing political control. One sees at once that thus they escaped from much time-exacting routine of state functions, and obtained leisure amid thought-provoking surroundings to work out problems of statecraft. But is there not another and even greater advantage to be obtained from a retirement into Nature that an overburdened ruler so shrewd as Charles could not fail to sense? The Greek legend of Antæus gaining renewed strength from the Earth every time he was thrown upon it is full of pregnant truth. The Charles that sat musing within his dainty garden was gaining from it just such mental refreshment against problems of empire government as Antæus received physically. "A quaint conceit," says the shrug of your shoulders, but be not too sure that this conceit is not one of those things that Hamlet urged were not dreamt of in his friend's philosophy—but nevertheless existed! If this conceit does no more than lure you to visit these winsome gardens and on into their heart where beats most audibly their ancient memories, "'tis enough, 'twill serve." Upon the delights of Moorish architecture as evidenced within the Alcázar, we shall not here enlarge, but shall wait until in the next chapter we reach Granada.

Charles V will not remain behind as we reluctantly leave his garden retreat and, refreshed in spirit through both eye and ear, cross over to the vast cathedral. We will enter by the portal at the right of the eastern end, close to where the mighty Giralda tower rises, and once inside turn about so as to see the window above the entrance. A fine portrait of Charles V confronts us, erect within a domed Renaissance archway of gorgeous glass, all carefully and brilliantly contrived. Strange, is it not, that so fragile a material as this should so long and safely serve as a memorial? And yet often it proves to have outlasted sterner stuff. Horace says that his poems are a monument more enduring than brass;—if he had lived any time after the 11th century, he might properly have employed a stained glass window for his simile instead of a brazen monument. If that ancient Roman were alive to-day, he would be amazed to learn that the only portrait extant of Prince Arthur, heir apparent of Henry VII of England, and brother of Henry VIII (who came to the throne by his death), is upon a much travelled window made in Holland, but finally lodged in St. Margaret's, Westminster. The only picture that has come down to us through the ages of the famous Golden Shrine of the martyred Thomas à Becket of Canterbury, appears on a 13th century panel in that cathedral. Its position proves that it must have been a faithful likeness, for it faced the shrine itself for centuries before Henry VIII looted it along with twenty-six cartloads of precious metals and jewels it possessed. The best portraits in existence of Constable Anne de Montmorency, his wife, and their twelve children, appear on four sets of windows in and near the town of his name near Paris.

Seville Cathedral has two surprises in store for one. Before ever the tourist enters the cathedral, having learned that it is only second to St. Peter's at Rome, he expects to be similarly impressed by a sense of sobering vastness, but he is not ! Also, because he has read of 93 ancient windows awaiting his inspection, he expects such a burst of coloured light as greets one on entering Leon Cathedral, or at least a sweeping *coup d'œil* from one spot as at Gerona, or from several, as at Toledo. But again realization reproves expectation. Within he will find a judiciously dim interior, seemingly all top-lighted and with but few windows visible from any one spot. The explanation of the disappointment in seeming vastness and also in abundance of coloured windows is largely the same, viz. up and down the middle of the interior are erected the great coro, which occupies so much space as to reduce its seeming size and also to shut off most of the windows from view, except those directly in front of you. Furthermore, the frequent bulky columns required to sustain the enormous roof hide most of the clerestory lights from any one viewpoint. Also the depths of the numerous chapels means that their protruding side-walls conceal all chapel windows save those of the one in front of which the observer happens to stand. This all means that one who enters here is inclined at first to conclude that there are fewer windows than at Segovia, Tarragona, or several other places. But it does not take long to convince one that Seville is peculiarly rich in ancient glass, and that too of the highest quality.

At what point shall we begin our inspection of this wealth of nearly a hundred mediæval windows ? Shall we scrupulously and intelligently proceed from the less interesting up to the superlative, as a child saves the most alluring dainty to be eaten last, or go systematically around like the benighted folk who are " personally conducted " through European galleries ? Why not cast reason and method aside, plunge headlong into this sea of colour, and snatch the best first ? And the best, the superlatively best, of all Spain is here. Here late windows with their Renaissance canopies and other architectural borders are so warmed by touches of pot-metal colour as to glow and glow with a fervour that never fades from out our memory. Where in all Europe can there be surpassed in sumptuous richness large scenes such as the gorgeous set around the clerestory above the north and south apse aisles ? Here on the north we have the pageantry of the Entry into Jerusalem, and dramatic episodes such as raising Lazarus from the dead and Magdalen washing the Saviour's feet ;—these in the north aisle clerestory. The backgrounds are light blue, a stronger blue being used with warm reds in the costumes. Generally they are divided into an upper and a lower section, with a saint presiding above over the scene or group below. Over on the southern side the clerestory above the apse aisle glows and glistens with the Last Supper, the Driving out of the Money Changers from the Temple, etc., etc. The detail throughout all these scenes is lavish in the extreme ; note the bunches of grapes festooned around within the upper arch above the Last Supper. Renaissance decorative detail is here raised to the nth power !

One of the many delights of stained glass hunting is that no two hunters can ever agree upon the order of excellence among their finds. This results in fruitful discussions among enthusiasts, and it is only a Trappist monk who cannot get joy out of a discussion. Just to start such a dispute, let the author announce that he prefers the gorgeous series around the apse aisles' clerestories just described, and then, next in order, the ojos de buey of the north and south transepts, followed by the St. Francis' chapel window and the Conversion of St. Paul next alongside. We admit that it is customary to praise highly the Cárlos Bruses windows facing each other in the north transept, but we beg repectfully to dissent ! Opposite to the Ascension is his Descent of the Holy Ghost, in the other wall of this transept. They are much better drawn than coloured, which happens seldom in Spain, but, fine as they are, should be content to fall in behind the list given above.

In passing it is amusing to notice how an incorrect interpretation of phrasing used by an early Spanish author in describing this Ascension as being over the door *of* the Capilla de las Doncellas has been the undoing of several lazy writers in both Spanish and English. The first of these borrowers of other men's work interpreted the word " of " to mean " in," thus making the Ascension scene a resident of the chapel aforesaid instead of being installed in the transept wall outside above the chapel. Thereupon an unobserving line of copyist authors have gone on describing this window as being inside the chapel instead of outside. Even Rico y Sinobas, the Spanish authority, makes this mistake, not once but twice, in his lives of Spanish glaziers. One cannot too highly praise the literary skill each used to camouflage his praise of the window so as to prevent us realizing he could never have looked upon it, since it has never occupied the place he describes !

As a matter of fact, the large window in the Capilla de las Doncellas contains an attractive Annunciation scene. The Virgin wears a gorgeous red gown and blue cloak, and in striking contrast thereto are the white garments of the women kneeling about her upon a pavement of light green and white tiles. This skilful swirl of white about a central feature of rich colour reminds one of the way in which Guglielmo di Marcillac obtains at Arezzo his mass effects by grouping costumes of contrasting hues.

In the order of excellence which, like the apple of Paris, we have presented above, there is included picture windows alone. Now let us venture another comment equally provocative of dispute, viz. we hold that in the southerly side of the chapel adjoining the east central one on the right, is one of the most delightful pattern windows in the world. It bears the date of 1789, so it is far later than any other fine window of ancient make. A large monogram in greenish-blue of M and A intertwined is enmeshed in shimmering cream strapwork, and all against a light blue background—fascinating in daintiness of tint and design. Especially observe the delicacy with which the

133

white straps and flowery details work out into golden hues toward the end of the garlands, and also the dark lines introduced round about to throw into bolder relief the faint tints employed. One can safely recommend that any glazier of to-day go all the way to Seville to study this gem of his craft,—it can hardly be surpassed as a teacher both of technique and effect.

After this rambling into by-paths let us return to our arbitrary order of excellence where next after the super-effective pictures along the clerestory above the north and south apse aisles came (in our humble opinion) the two ample bull's eyes or ojos de buey swung high in the ends of the north and south transepts. In the northern one a horizontal band of deep blue sky across the middle separates the ascending Christ (amid yellowish clouds) from His sorrowing disciples below, where blue, red, and yellow strive for pre-eminence. At the south, the composition of the picture is more graceful. The Virgin sits enthroned just above the ojo's centre, and again there is much blue sky, but not so deep in hue as opposite, and the division it provides is not so definitely horizontal, but sweeps gently upwards at the ends. Here the blue, except in the sky, yields frankly to a predominance of red and yellow, except for an almost black robe in the lower right centre.

And now to conclude our list of ordered excellence before making a general round of the cathedral, let us turn to St. Francis' chapel and its neighbour containing the Conversion of St. Paul. The St. Francis chapel is the eastmost on the north side of the nave, next against the north transept. The picture is boldly drawn, to a large scale, but is chiefly interesting for the excellence of colour and also for the deft combination of red and gold in its elaborate golden Renaissance framing. This latter is distinctly Spanish, and the date is 1556. The central figure is St. Francis in a light brown robe, kneeling. It is difficult to decide which is more pleasing—the picture or its gorgeous frame. In the next chapel to the west is the much praised Conversion of St. Paul, dated 1560. Perhaps we will agree that its most interesting feature is the marching soldiery through the green woods that form the background. Their partial concealment increases their apparent number. A bearded St. Paul lies thrown upon his back in the foreground. The woolly beards of several figures round about him remind one of Baldovinetti's work in the window over the altar of the Pazzi chapel adjoining Santa Croce in Florence.

And now for a comprehensive tour about the interior. We might as well follow on from where we find ourselves, and comment upon the nave chapels, which, however, will not detain us long after having seen the two best just described. The next chapel to their west is modern glazed, and next beyond is one with a 1683 window, of interest because containing so early a picture of the famous Giralda tower close by outside. New Yorkers are familiar with this tower because at Madison Square Garden they have one which follows it closely except in the slenderer proportions of the modern adaptation. All the nave chapel embrasures are broad single ones. Across on the south side of the nave, the westmost is as much too heavily coloured as its neighbour to the east (1797) is too faintly. The next two are both of 1819, and both uninteresting, as is likewise the fifth and eastmost, of modern glazing.

The nave aisle clerestory windows, five on the north side and four on the south, have four lancets, a single saint in each, but with too much blue background above and below the figures within their lofty Gothic canopies.

Much more interesting than these lower ones are the real clerestory lights that further inward run along above them. Here within each group, again of four lancets, are graceful late Gothic canopies, each canopy running across a pair of lancets. One receives the impression that the figures in the canopies are much older than the blue background, but perhaps this only means too much restoration of certain parts. Note in the eastmost on the north side the sumptuous effect produced by a magenta damask curtain suspended across the back of two lancets, with a blue damask one across the other pair.

The western façade is admirably lighted. High up in the centre is a large rose of a twelve-petalled design with a roomy ojo at its core, in which are installed the four Evangelists. Over the small portal at the right and left of this façade is a modest ojo with a larger ojo de buey between it and the great dominating roseton. A Visitation (1777) fills the northerly of the two larger ojos and a much earlier Annunciation the southerly one. Unfortunately, there is usually suspended across the two

larger ojos and the great roseton dark curtains to shut
off the strong afternoon light, lest it flood the nave,
tempered though it be by colour. Sometimes these
curtains are drawn aside, but this is not easy to arrange.
Spanish priests treat with courtesy those who show
an intelligent interest in their churches. Unfortunately, this same courteous microbe does not
infect the lay attendants at Seville, who suffer
instead from dyspepsia of the disposition.

Proceeding on our inspection, we now reach
the transepts and find continued around into them
the single saints under canopies that are stationed
along the nave clerestory, and at the same level.
Some of these transept clerestory embrasures have
three lancets, but generally there are four, and always
they culminate in tracery lights above. The
transepts protrude only one bay to the north and
south beyond the side walls of the nave and apse
chapels, and in this bay there is, on a level with
the aisle clerestory of the nave, a tall single lancet,
except in the west wall of the south transept, where
it is blocked up. It is these two lancets facing
each other in the north transept which contain
Cárlos Bruses' Ascension and Descent of the Holy
Ghost already mentioned.

The cimborio above the crossing seems far, far above us, and this perspective of distance is enhanced by the smallness of the two windows each of three lancets which on all four sides of the cimborio fit down snugly upon the supporting arch.

And now for that portion of the church lying east of the crossing. Beginning on the highest level, we notice that of the clerestory embrasures piercing the three bays on each side, the central ones, just above the stately retablo, are walled up. We have already remarked how excellent is the most easterly window on the south side—strikingly rich and fine.

Dropping down and outward on each side we reach the clerestory lights above the apse aisles, one broad one to each of the three bays, both on the north and south. Each is unincumbered with mullions, and its whole space given over to gorgeous glass in the best Renaissance manner, and is ranked by us ahead of all others here.

Very fine indeed is the manner in which the architect has fashioned the easterly end of his structure. Three chapels extend outward, the central (and larger) one further than the two shallower which flank it. In all there are windows, and others are added to the wall itself above the side portals to the north and south. Generally speaking, the glazing at this end is not so satisfactory as elsewhere round the church, although it ranks above the later windows along the south side nave chapels. Exception, however, must be made in favour of two windows already praised,— the portrait of Charles V over the northerly portal, and the delicious confection of 1789 counterfeiting spider-web and dew, in the southerly of the two small chapels. In the eastern embrasures of the northerly small chapel is much the oldest glass here, a dark-visaged St. Peter with salmon-pink halo and key, attired in a red, blue, and green robe. This was probably brought from an earlier church, and needed a much later border to fill out its new emplacement. The purple background is also obviously much later than the central figure.

Most of the glass in Seville Cathedral speaks Spanish with a strong Flemish accent ! It is unusually fine work of its period and, begun in 1504 by Micer Christóbal Aleman, was carried forward without pause by him and his successors during the first and best three-quarters of that amazingly artistic century. Money was spent freely by the Chapter upon its windows, as many items in their records attest, and there is absolutely no doubt that the glazing we to-day so intensely enjoy was considered by contemporary taste to be the highest expression then reached by stained glass. After a considerable lapse of time came the later windows to which we have referred without enthusiasm.

In the south transept is the sarcophagus containing the mortal remains of Christopher Columbus, borne aloft by heroic figures in bronze representing the Kingdoms of Castile, Aragon, Leon, and Navarre. It is significantly symbolic that these giant porters seem always ready to set forth upon a journey with their precious burden, for already it has greatly travelled. After the death of the famous explorer, his remains were brought from Valladolid and buried in Nuestra Señora de las Cuevas, across the river from Seville. They lay there from 1509 until 1540, when they were exhumed and transported to Santo Domingo, where they were allowed to rest until 1796, when they were transferred to the Cathedral of Havana. When Cuba became a free Republic in 1898, his remains, enclosed and supported as they are to-day, were finally removed to their present site. "Peace to his ashes," most reverently say we Americans, who owe so much to his enterprising wanderings.

The Spaniards say "whom God loves, He gives a house in Seville." That happy man should choose one in the Calle de las Sierpes, the street of the serpents, a friendly lane of unfriendly name, a narrow leisurely thoroughfare where vehicles may not intrude, and whose crowds never jostle as they stroll between the shops and clubs that line it.

GRANADA

ALGEBRA, as its name indicates, was invented by the Arabs, and as for geometry, if you wish to see it in blossom, you have only to turn to Moorish architecture in Spain—Mudejar, as the Spaniards call it. Nothing at all copied after living nature, not even symbolically, as the Gothic hints of branching trees in the forest, or Greek columns of bare tree trunks. Not even such floral hints as the frozen acanthus leaves of the Corinthian capitals in the ultimate development of the Greek. No, the Moor strictly followed the injunctions of the Koran and in no wise made graven images of living things, thereby obeying his Scriptures more scrupulously than do many Christians who disregard the Second Commandment by having images of all sorts in their churches. No, Moorish architecture, always charmingly light and graceful, and sometimes almost ethereal in its loveliness, is nothing more or less than geometrical design or structure logically developed. A certain

Frenchman, Bourgouin by name, divides all art and architecture into Arabic, Greek, and Japanese. For him, the Japanese represents the vegetable kingdom, Greek the animal kingdom, and Arabic the mineral, because its structure so closely follows the shapes of the geometrical crystals into which minerals naturally fall.

Nor was the bounteous gift of beauty with which Moorish architecture blessed Spain its only benefaction, for also there was Moorish administration of government. The Koran enjoins spreading the Faith by the sword, so perhaps it is not surprising that in only one hundred years after Mahomet's death in 632 the Crescent swept across Africa, conquered all of the Spanish peninsula, and pressed forward to meet the final check to its flood-tide before Tours at the hands of Charles Martel in 733. Amazing as such wide and rapid conquest seems, it is as nothing in comparison with the convincing excellence of governmental administration that accompanied it. In 710 the Moorish general Tarik crossed over the Straits from Africa to a great rock ever since known by his name, Gebel-al-Tarik, the mountain of Tarik, Gibraltar! In eight months thereafter he had taken the Visigothic capital of Toledo, and in that short time had overthrown their empire which had lasted for centuries. And now came the most surprising result of that swooping conquest. Was it difficult for the Moor to hold in subjection all this wide territory with forces strong enough for raiding warfare, but surely inadequate for extensive garrisoning? It was not, and for the striking reason that Moorish rule was equitable in the extreme and satisfied the people. Not only was it just and fair to the conquered inhabitants in matters of civil jurisdiction, but also was it equally tolerant in permitting both Christians and Jews to worship God each in his own fashion—in amazing contrast to the tyranny of the Visigoths that preceded Moslem rule, and the Holy Inquisition that followed it! In matters relating to the advancement of learning, Spanish Moors were far in advance of their time. Their schools and the University of Cordova were justly renowned all over Europe, and the latter's pre-eminent contributions to the higher learning lasted from about 750 until its conquest by the Christians in 1236. It is not pleasant for a Christian to make these admissions, but facts must be faced. The Moorish control of the Peninsula, begun in 711, was not broken until the great battle of Las Navas de Tolosa in 1212. By 1238 their control was wrested from them, although the province of Granada continued under Moslem government until 1492, a date easy for an American to remember. Then the Crescent was definitely and finally expelled from the Peninsula, and with it went much learning and incidentally the finest architectural inspiration the country has ever enjoyed.

It is no part of this book's purpose to describe the fascination of the Alhambra, but Americans may well take honest pride in the fact, recognized by all Spaniards, that it was our Washington Irving who, by his charming tales of this Moorish Palace, caused steps to be taken for its preservation and restoration. It was while he was American Minister to Spain that he abode many weeks inside the Alhambra enclosure writing those delightful chronicles. Taken with John Hay's " Castilian Days " they form a literary monument to American diplomacy only equalled elsewhere by Motley's histories of Holland, written while American Minister to The Hague. Would that our politicians permitted us to have more such men in our diplomatic service !

ANCIENT MUDEJAR OR MOORISH WINDOWS

Old Synagogue, Toledo.   These windows were not glazed at all, or else had their traceries backed by a plate of white
glass or alabaster

But even if there were no Alhambra in Granada, nor any Generalife Gardens, vieing in their Moorish lure with the palace opposite them, still we would have taken our tourists thither. Granada's cathedral possesses fine windows, not only of an excellent period but also in quantity equalling their quality. The two better hotels are up the hill close by the Alhambra, and in one of them I heard an American lady say to the porter, " I want to buy some hairpins ; must I go down to the village for them ? " Well, it is down into what she styled the village, the city of Granada built on the plain below the high-perched Alhambra, that we must go for the cathedral and its glass.

Fortunately for their effect, all the forty-four ancient windows are assembled in one part of the interior, around the apse ambulatory, and up in the apse dome, above and around the high altar. Unfortunately, however, they are very high up, so much so as to make opera glasses almost a necessity if one wishes to spell out the details of their stories. Those in the dome are finer than their cousins of the apse ambulatory, indeed are among the very finest in all Spain, which is saying a good deal. All this Granada glass is of the ripest Renaissance period, mid-16th century, and for richness both of colour and detail cannot well be surpassed.

Around the apse ambulatory swing in a curve twenty-two windows, all let into the wall above the chapels, and stationed in groups of three, separated by a single light. The central one bears the date 1550. The treatment is the same all around this series—a single figure in deep colour heavily framed after the Renaissance manner in much gold framing. One feels, however, that the colouring of both frame and figure are thicker than they need be.

With the dome windows no such comment is possible, for here we have colour of the happiest and golden Renaissance framing of the most brilliant type. The gold is pure gold, and the reds are rich and strong, but the blues, especially in the sky backgrounds, are of tenderest tint. The placing of these delightful windows is quite unique and resembles nothing seen anywhere else. The dome is ceiled with a circular cupola, and just below it run all the way round ten wide, round-arched windows. Below this circling crown of light runs another, but not all the way round, as the front or westerly side gives way to make room for the top of the arch coming up from below. These lower lights, also round arched, are not so large as the upper ones, and are grouped in pairs, each pair stationed below one of the upper ones, in perfect triangular balance. Of this lower row there are fourteen, so that only seven of the upper ones has its pair of supporters underneath, the three west-most lacking them because of the arch arising from below. The colour scheme throughout is the same, both above and below. The drawing of these scenes is admirable and repays careful in-spection through opera glasses. Perhaps we shall decide that the three best are the central eastmost ones in the upper row, showing respectively Christ carrying the Cross, the Crucifixion, and the Descent from the Cross. So high up are these windows that there is room below them not only for a series of lofty and wide-framed paintings, but also lower down, a gallery which runs round above the arched openings into the apse ambulatory. Of course we understand that top lighting is necessary in this climate, especially so far south in Spain, but here it seems carried to an extreme. It is really a pity that such fine glass pictures should not be nearer the eye of the observer.

The wise way for the glass tourist to visit

Granada is to go out to it by train, nine hours from Seville, or else come straight from Madrid, eleven hours, and return by Seville. The author, however, made the mistake of going by train to Malaga and from thence 128 kilometres over the mountains to Granada. He was misled by an old book that told of ancient glass in Malaga Cathedral, which, alas! no longer exists. But he is glad of the mistake, because of the wonderful ride over the mountains from Malaga to Loja, 76 kilometres. Especially glorious was the first 16 kilometres out from Malaga, during which you rise 1000 metres, with ever-changing views below you of the city and the sea. The 52 kilometres from Loja into Granada is flat, uninteresting, and badly surfaced. As usual in Spain, the mountain roads, fine pieces of engineering skill, are better kept up than those in the plains.

This interesting trip lets one see much of the olive and cane culture around Malaga, and then when one gets over the mountains into the province of Granada, the sugar-beet industry there so prevalent and profitable.

Coming this way into Granada one has an impressive view of the Alhambra, stationed high up on a spur of the hills in front, smiling sadly down upon what was once a great Moorish capital. The Spaniards with justice call this view, seen from the opposite hill, " El Ultimo Suspiro del Moro," for this was the last sight that the expelled Moors had of their beloved and entrancing home.

Apropos of misleading accounts in old books concerning ancient glass no longer to be seen, it may be well to add here that correspondence with local sacristans reveals that the mediæval glazing is gone from Ciudad Rodrigo, Jeréz, Santiago de Campostello, Valencia, and Zamora.

A centripetal force, like the force of gravity, draws us back to Madrid, and yet Madrid is not famed for gravity ! To this force we must once more yield after leaving the glass of Seville and Granada to see that of Catalonia. All day back to Madrid from Granada, or all night from Seville, and then all night again to Barcelona. Fortunately, night trains in Spain are comfortable, starting at a reasonable hour after the day's occupations, and arriving at an equally reasonable one for breakfast. A certain New York poet once said, " Cursed be he who first invented and went about advising that artificial cut off early rising."

BARCELONA

WHEN autumn and winter begin to close in upon Europe, then memories of the Riviera recommence their siren song, and the flood tide of travel sets in toward that favoured strip of Mediterranean foreshore, where the mountains cut off the north winds, the sun smiles and the sea sparkles. Florida has the same lure for Americans of the north at the same time of year and for similar reasons. The province of Catalonia, fronting on the Mediterranean, and buttressed by the Pyrenees on the north and a coastal range along the west, is for the rest of Spain both Riviera and Florida, plus California's all-year climate thrown in for good measure. Add to all this, that its capital, Barcelona, the largest of Spanish cities (nearly a million inhabitants), is one of the brightest, most active, and go-ahead cities in all Europe. Picturesque too, for nothing can exceed the beauty of the panorama spread out below one perched on the high platform

152

atop Mount Tibidabo, that bold elevation that
obligingly rises just back of the city, and up which
one mounts by a spectacular funicular or by an
even more spectacular motor road of pleasing
perfection. Stand there towards sunset, and watch
the shadows lengthen across the fertile Catalonian
valleys to the right and left, whilst below you the
city lights begin to twinkle out, with the history-
laden Mediterranean beyond for a background,—
a spectacle one never forgets ! Or take a sunny
morning (and Catalonia's year has many such) on
the Rambla, that most engaging of streets, a broad
tree-shaded walk down its centre, festooned on both
sides by flower booths, and flanked by driveways
and enticing shop windows. Here Señor Don
Everyman meets Señora and Señorita Everybody
Else for a frank and even exchange of views and
gossip. Stocks of good humour are replenished
and trade therein encouraged. You really must
come to Barcelona because we want to show you
its interesting glass, but it is worth your while to
go there even if you be not of our artistic guild,
if only to see this progressive city cutting through
new boulevards but preserving its ancient architectural heirlooms. If you wish to witness the

hustle of modern Spanish enterprise, here it is best to be seen. But if you are fleeing from hustle at home and want *dolce far niente* of the most idle sort, our prescription is for you to step in from a certain busy Barcelona street into the charming cloisters adjoining its cathedral. Drop down upon a seat and give yourself over to the charm of the quaint carvings, the soothing green of this sequestered court, and the stately tower which for centuries has looked down approvingly on just such idlers as you wish to be. Here in this soothing retreat you will find monotony relieved by the constant stream of passers-by interrupting their day's occupation for a brief prayer in the sanctuary beyond, for Catalans seem more devout than all other Spaniards. The author has spent many hours in cathedrals and churches in all parts of Spain and has been surprised to find how meagre was the attendance even at choral services, but in Catalonia the opposite is true. Even if two services are being held at the same time before different altars in the same church, and this happens often in Barcelona, both will be well attended. The largest congregation anywhere remarked was in Tarragona Cathedral.

Not only does the Barcelona Cathedral possess treasures of ancient glass but so also do the churches of Santa Maria del Mar and Santa Maria del Pino. The finest craftsmanship of the glazier will be seen at the Cathedral, but the most interesting display at Santa Maria del Mar. It is well to be frank at the outset, by admitting that Barcelona glass is generally crude in design and colouring, but our tourist will surely come to admit that there is about its crudity a certain robustness,—a quality of early vigour that lays hold upon the imagination. This crudity pertains to Barcelona alone and not to its two neighbours, Tarragona and Gerona.

In the Cathedral we shall obtain our greatest satisfaction from the range of windows which run around the apse above the chapels but below the clerestory lights. They seem to date themselves partly as late in the 16th century and partly as early in the 15th. Very entertaining is the artist's conceit in placing an over-large rooster just below his small St. Peter conventionally ensconced in a modest Gothic canopy—" lest we forget ! " This embrasure is enlivened by many shields bearing the red and yellow upright bars of Catalonia, seen also in the tracery lights above. Next on the right is a fine Virgin within a 14th century canopy, with a Crucifixion scene just above. About her, in the side lancets, we have a modest and artistic method of advertising the donor—a series of handsomely emblazoned lozenges indicating that a lady of the Despujols family was the benefactress. The small mountain with a blossom at the top (to the uninitiate rather resembling a bell) decorates the design and enlightens the beholder at the same time, and yet does not intrude upon the picture as donors elsewhere so frequently do. All through this series of apse windows may be remarked geometric patterns made of variously coloured bits of glass, a fashion very popular in Germany in those days. These same patterns are frequent in all the glazing of this Cathedral. But perhaps we may feel that their colour is too often strong without being rich. On the south side of the nave the third embrasure from the end has within its late (15th century) Gothic canopies and behind the single figure of each lancet, a background that recalls the plaid of a Scottish clan, so strong are the contrasting hues there checkered,—green and brown, red and white.

There is not room for a rose window in the west

façade, so low down comes the ample eight-sided cimborio or lantern that so pleasingly lights the western portion of the interior. Down in the north-west corner of this façade is the Baptistery, and although its window is attributed to Bermejo and is therefore praised, it is doubtful if we shall admire the colouring or design of the two lancets which, taken together, form one picture. On the north side of the nave the two eastmost embrasures of four lancets each show a graceful treatment of coloured shields across grisaille, all within gay borders. The lighting of the Cathedral is almost entirely from above, and though decidedly dim, is appropriate to its period and its climate.

Much brighter, too bright say many Catalans, is the interior of Santa Maria del Pino. Here we have no nave or transepts ; not even rudimentary transepts like those at the Cathedral,—simply one single, sweeping space. Above on each side are six large embrasures of three lancets each, topped off with decorated tracery lights, while below are six shallow chapels on each side. Around the curved apse of the east end are five large windows. The first and third in each side wall counting from the west are the best. The first in the south wall shows a combination of soft green and white and a moderate amount of blue, with touches of brown picking out the pavement below the figures. Facing it in the north wall is a similar colour scheme, but here there is added some reddish-brown in the costumes. The third in the south wall has one scene running across all four lancets in its upper half, while below, each lancet contains a single figure in a crude canopy. Facing it across the church is a rather extraordinary Nativity, the sky of which is done in checkered brown and white lozenges in whose midst shines the Star of Bethlehem ! But the chief glory of the church is the great rose window in the west wall, full of coloured geometric patterns. It is difficult to say which is the more admirable—its colour seen from within, or its graceful petal-like framework best studied from the outside.

Midway between the airy lightness of Santa Maria del Pino, dangerously near to a glare on a bright day, and the intentional gloom within the Cathedral, is the illumination found at Santa Maria del Mar. Midway also is its interior construction between the utter simplicity of Santa Maria del Pino and the division into the usual nave, transepts, and apse shown at the Cathedral, for at Santa Maria del Mar we have the simple nave, but an ambulatory around the apse, plus a suggestion of transepts. Here there is more ancient glazing than at both its rivals put together, and richer in tone though cruder in design. Best of all is the large rose window in the middle of the western façade. In the centre of its framework is an ojo with a seated figure in strong reds and greens from which radiate golden rays. Flanking this rose on either side is stationed a tall grouping of three lancets, the central one occupied by a single figure lacking, however, the usual canopy, the side lancets containing the coloured patterns so popular in Barcelona. The single saints which people so many of the lancets along the side walls inhabit canopies distinctly crude in their drawing. In fact, the drawing in this church is everywhere so secondary to the colour scheme as often to make it difficult to spell out the story. Especially is this true of the second from the west on the north side of the nave, which is meant for the Last Supper, beneath whose light green pyramidal roof are grouped golden haloed figures. This and its neighbour to the east are the two most interesting windows here. The latter depicts the Last Judgment, and the red fire at the bottom of its right-hand lancet is most convincing ! Striking, too, is the green at the bottom of the three other lancets, from which arise many praying figures, all facing God the Father seated at the top of the right central lancet ; —clearly a Resurrection Day. Around the apse are nine tall embrasures in which the maker of geometrical coloured patterns has been given a free hand ;—perhaps our reader will find this an understatement ! Of the interesting glazing in this church it is fair to comment " strong colour but rude drawing." All of which means that here is an interior that it is well to visit just before twilight, when the light is beginning to fail. Try it some day, and you will be well repaid.

Doubtless all who use Barcelona as a centre for viewing Catalan glass, will first take the short run out to San Cugal del Vallés, which, if desired, can be fitted into a longer trip to the famous mountain shrine of Montserrat. Although Montserrat is of interest to students of Parsifal and the Holy Grail legend, and a most delightful motor excursion, it unfortunately lacks stained glass. The two recommended glass jaunts are, one to the north, two hours by train (the motor road is bad), to Gerona, and the other south to Tarragona, a hundred kilometres by a road partly excellent, partly bad, or two hours by train. For most people the Tarragona visit will probably precede that to Gerona, because the latter is on the direct road back to nearby France. Many tourists who enter Spain by Irun like to vary their experiences by leaving it around the other or eastern end of the Pyrenees, which to us means via Gerona.

SAN CUGAL DEL VALLÉS

WE have already spoken of the splendid panorama of Barcelona, the sea, and the Catalan foreshore that unrolls itself before and below an observer perched on Mount Tibidabo. If we ascend that height by its motor road, a triumph of engineering skill, this panorama will be unfolded to us in ever developing chapters as we pass around corner after corner of the broad and easy ascent. Not far from the top is a fork in the road ; a turn to the left leads to the mountain's nearby summit, but let us instead turn to the right and follow around the shoulder of the hill to where the descent begins, yielding a new series of views, this time inland ones. Over fertile and picturesque valleys and across wooded slopes we shall espy the serrated crest of Montserrat, that abruptly lofty fastness credited by the Middle Ages with being the hiding-place of the Holy Grail, so anxiously and prayerfully sought by many a feudal knight. Still further beyond lies the noble background of the Pyrenees, sturdy bulwark of the Hispanic countries.

Winding down and ever down, we shall finally come to the town of San Cugal del Vallés, only a score of kilometres from Barcelona. There are few more picturesque motor rides in the world than this one, and it seems excessive generosity which provides a charming stained glass shrine at the end of a golden chain of such scenic delights. To the author's mind, one has to go all the way to Hong-kong in order to rival in beauty this motor run of only three-quarters of an hour.

Entering the small village church we shall observe that during the 15th century its already ancient western façade was pierced to receive an overpoweringly large rose window. Somehow, to one coming from Barcelona, it has a familiar look, and after a little study of its parti-coloured glass patterns, and especially of the graceful petal-shaped stone traceries that methodically divide the whole into twelve intermingling zones, we suddenly conclude that here is a near kin to the western roseton of Santa Maria del Pino. Obviously the same architect and the same glazier worked hand and hand in both these churches. This San

Cugal rose window is no less than nine yards across, but this means that what seems but a reasonably proportioned window in the roomy Barcelona church is here, for a small interior, almost overpowering. It fills the entire width between the interior columns, and occupies fully half the height from floor to ceiling. A perfect monster of a window,—almost unmercifully adorning so modest sized an edifice. It is flamboyant Gothic at its best, but notwithstanding all its beauty, it teaches a significant lesson anent the ever-present necessity of proportion in decoration.

The Catalans call this town San Cugat instead of San Cugal, a geographical reminder that throughout all this region there is much interest in preserving the Catalan speech, an old dialect midway between Spanish and French, which even to-day preserves a vigorous literature both in prose and poetry.

If the tourist continues on to make the delightful pilgrimage up Montserrat, do not let him be misled by guide-books (as was the writer) into believing there is fine stained glass at Manresa, not far beyond the base of Montserrat. The motor road leading thither is enticingly good, but the glass is modern !

TARRAGONA

ASHORE road always means an opportunity for beauty, whether it winds about
within sight of an open sea, or along
the bank of a river with views of its partner
across the dividing water. The mere mention of
such a road recalls pleasant memories,—of the
Corniche above Monte Carlo, of the drive up the
Hudson, of the Szechenyi road along the Danube
above the Iron Gates, of sundry panoramic ways
beside the Pacific in California, Oregon, or Hawaii,
etc. Such another is that from Barcelona, one
hundred kilometres south to Tarragona. Parts of
it are over fertile plains that undulate down to the
sea, but also long stretches are blasted out from the
sheer cliffs with nothing below but the blue waves
of the Mediterranean, as smiling and peaceful on
most days of the year as if this inland sea had not
for centuries been the cockpit of international strife.
And which of all the warrior nations of the Mediterranean has not during its supremacy laid hold upon

this desirable Catalonian coast land! At Tarragona their history is written in stone, yes, and even back of history lies the beginnings of the record, for prehistoric are the huge cyclopean blocks that lie along the base of its ancient walls. Nothing is known of those early builders, able to handle such masses of rock so dexterously. Much later came the Greeks, recognizing the strategic value of Tarragona's lofty site, so conveniently close to the beach as to double its value for a people that went "down to the sea in ships, and occupied their business in great waters." Here came the Carthaginians, and through its streets echoed the heavy tramp of elephants on their way to help Hannibal conquer distant Rome far off around those blue waters. He failed, and the Roman victors replaced Carthaginian supremacy in Tarragona, then become a valued outpost of the ever-spreading Roman Empire. Nearby is the fine Roman aqueduct, only rivalled in Spain by that of Segovia. Here too came the conquering Moslem, long to be master of these fortified heights. To defeat him was so crucial a task that its accomplishment proved the making of the Spanish nation.

You will soon come to agree that the security of

Tarragona is a truly agreeable one, so pleasing is the outlook from its terraces over the sea, and so picturesque the rambles through its devious streets. Up and up we go to where the Cathedral crowns its highest point. And what a Cathedral ! So impressive within and without, and with this impressiveness such charm ! Alongside nestle the delightful cloisters where, shaded, one may stroll about the refreshing green of the inner patio, stopping now and again to decipher mediæval legends on its ancient walls or, if sufficiently learned, certain early Moslem inscriptions narrating that here the faith of Mahomet long held sway.

Most of the stained glass here—and there is much—dates from the second half of the 16th century, but also there is a great deal of what an Irishman might call "glazing without glass," which, being interpreted, means the filling of embrasures with pierced stone slabs instead of sheets of glass. This is to be seen in the transepts, along the clerestory of the nave, but best in the eight embrasures, half of three and half of four lancets, around the cimborio or lantern which high above the transepts crowns the crossing. The apertures, round or square, that pierce these stone slabs, are filled with coloured

167

glass, which, if we consider the slabs an apology for glazing, make a distinctly handsome apology. Their use materially modifies the illumination, which always gave concern to a Spanish architect. We have already remarked that at Valencia and Sagunto we may see slabs, this time of alabaster, used for this same purpose of subduing excessive sunlight, but to see this method at its best, one must repair to certain Italian churches such as San Miniato (above Florence) or Orvieto. Sit before an alabaster window at sunset and watch the changing of its hues as the light dies out—a delicious experience !

The finest stained glass here is in the great rose windows that adorn the ends of the transepts. They are credited to Juan Guas, and are dated 1574. The southern one is much the better, for its northern brother suffers from injudicious restoration, plus some frank replacement of old with new. In the centre of each rose is a sixfoil opening ;—the southern one contains a seated Virgin in the central space with her feet upon a crescent moon which is adroitly fitted into the lowest cusp of the sixfoil, her head occupying the topmost one, and a miniature cherub each of the other four—skilful co-operation of glazier and stonemason, this ! The effect of colour in this rose is particularly brilliant. A large part of the north rose is given over to coloured geometric patterns, so frequent here. Each rose has sixteen large petals, and the broadest part of each petal contains a bust within a medallion border of contrasting hues ; several of these busts are missing from the north rose.

Around the apse are narrow Romanesque slits filled with old coloured patterns. At the east end behind the handsome retablo there projects a small Lady chapel lighted by one window, where St. Margaret tramples on a prostrate dragon, against an uncoloured quarry background, all within a gay border. There are more such quarries in the small chapel snuggled east of the north transept and north of the apse. Here are two small pairs of lancets housing late 14th century saints under canopies, with uncoloured quarry lights above and below them, and gay tracery lights to top them off. Note that each saint has a white written scroll alongside him—it is unusual in Spain, but is a decorative motif that was justifiably popular with German glaziers.

Starting west from the crossing, look up at the clerestory of the nave, and the fourth embrasure from the west on each side will show you fine old white grisaille, perhaps the best in all Spain. Several of the clerestory lights, particularly the three westmost on each side, are blocked with pierced stone slabs, in the manner already described.

On each side of the nave are five chapels, and most of their glass is ancient, even though in some places composed only of old fragments. The eastmost chapel on the south side has a large oval of grisaille strapwork of unusually broad straps against a varying background of blue, red, etc. Next to the west is more old grisaille, this time within gay borders and bearing blazoned escutcheons.

All this has brought us nearer to the west façade, where a treat awaits us, so well balanced and original is its treatment. An ample rose window above in the centre, and below a unique triangular embrasure capping the great west portal, while to right and left are medium-sized sixfoil lights, one with an ojo in its centre, the other without. Original, too, is the glazing of the great rose of florid Gothic, over thirty feet across,—all ancient grisaille, brightened by red objects which might be described as floating starfish, in default of some better term. Very cool and bright is this union of soft white and definite red, and right cunningly combined too, both in the roseton above and the large triangular transom light below it and above the wide portal. The forty-eight ancient windows of Tarragona Cathedral certainly leave a charmingly varied picture in one's memory.

SANTAS CREUS

TWENTY-FIVE miles inland from Tarragona, and near to Poblet on the route to Lerida, is Santas Creus, where may be seen a tall and ample window of several lancets, each one containing a series of small scenes one above another. It has recently been restored, fortunately with artistic judgment. The road is bad and there is only one window to be seen, so the foregoing may be taken rather as a note than a recommendation.

Another note having to do with Catalan glass to be seen from Barcelona as a centre, is as follows :— The Superintendent of the Instituto de Estudios Catalanes in Barcelona told the writer that at Santa Maria de Palantordera, which can be visited *en route* for Gerona, there are a few 17th century windows which he styled " unimportant."

He also said that at Cervera, not far from Lérida, are some small 16th century windows, interesting but not important.

GERONA

ONE of the pleasantest surprises in Spain were the delightful windows found in the great Cathedral at Gerona. They are mentioned by no writer, Spaniard or foreigner. Not even in nearby Barcelona did those in authority upon matters Catalan and artistic know anything of them. Their existence was indicated to the author by King Alfonso of Spain during his visit to Deauville in August, 1922. The King's second son, born in 1908, bears the title of Duca de Gerona. Not only are there plenty of ancient windows in this sturdy pile, twenty-nine of them, but also they are so disposed as to make a most pleasing display. If our traveller will take his stand by the gate into the chapel on the north side of the nave, just east of the corridor leading off to the cloisters, and face east by south, he will gaze upon an ensemble of mediæval glazing which only Leon can surpass in all Spain. Seen from this point, the organ will block sight of certain modern glass in the south wall

173

of the nave, and there will be left a prospect of ancient glass alone, finely coloured and handsomely grouped. Indeed, it is difficult to recall a more effective grouping of windows anywhere.

So excellent are the proportions of this tremendous nave that it comes rather as a surprise to learn how enormous it really is. Its width of 74 feet, when compared with the 52 feet at York Minster, or 49 at Cologne Cathedral, or 48 at Nôtre Dame in Paris, can at first hardly be realized. It is no wonder that its Chapter was at first aghast when that daring architect, Guilliermo Boffiy, proposed such dimensions for a nave which in 1416 he began to build in addition to the older apse of the preceding century. Needless to say, such a width necessitated a considerable height to balance it, which means that much wall space must rise at the east above the junction with the older and modester apse and ambulatory. How to adorn this upper eastern wall without attracting to it undue attention was indeed a problem. But it was handsomely met by inserting in the centre an enormous ojo de buey, larger even than that of the west wall, while supporting it, both right and left, above the unpierced triforium gallery, is another

ample circular opening, each handsomely filled
with a grouping of four sixfoil lights whose graceful
traceries contain rich early geometric patterns.

The ojo's wide coloured border bears golden
designs on a green background, with narrow edgings
all around of blue and brown. Within, upon old
greyish grisaille, is a large winged St. Michael,
mostly blue and brown, with a small round blue
and gold targe in his left hand. So poor is the
drawing that at first sight one does not grasp that
the saint is engaged in slaying a beast at his feet.
Unsatisfactory also is the picture filling the great
western ojo de buey, the only embrasure in that
façade. Again we have a single figure of late
glazing ; it looks like 17th century.

At the right of the great ensemble which we
noticed from our selected viewpoint are two large
windows in the south wall. They are unusually
lofty, so much so as to permit three full tiers of
good-sized canopied saints, one above the other.
The eastmost is the better, with tall Gothic pinnacles
handsomely finishing off the canopies. Its westerly
neighbour has canopies in the 16th century classical
style, but both for colour and drawing its figures are
surpassed by the first mentioned. There is a third

lofty window completing this series on the west, but it, like similar embrasures across the nave, contains modern glass.

The oldest part of the Cathedral is the apse and ambulatory finished in 1346, and beautifully lighted from above by a series of ten windows around the apse ambulatory and another of eleven around the apse clerestory. There are no windows in the apse chapels. The ambulatory ones are all of three lancets each, with a handsome triangular triplet of sixfoil tracery lights surmounting each group. They give a broader lighting than the clerestory series, narrower and crowded more closely together. The first ambulatory light on the right is modern glazed. A brief study of the others shows that the next two are by one artist, the next four by another, and the next three by a third, and yet they make a harmonious series. Much interest as well as instruction may be obtained from comparisons like this one. Note the green in the backgrounds, unusual at that time. There are also a few instances of double tiers of saints within mid-14th century canopies.

Moving up from the ambulatory series to the one of eleven stationed around the clerestory, it is at once clear that we are dealing with the 14th century and not later than its middle, because there is no yellow stain, discovered during its early years. Where yellow is needed here, even in the Gothic canopies, separate bits of a brassy yellow are leaded in. Also notice that green is used quite as much as red or blue in the canopies, another indication of the early days of that century. Generally the treatment here followed is that of a single figure under canopy in each lancet, and below another tier of saints but without canopies. The first light on the right has three tiers of them, one above the other. The most easterly seven are of two lancets each, the other four of three. Observe that two of the windows on the right are intended to be taken together, for thus they make up a Nativity. This is unusual for this century in any country, but is sometimes seen, as for example in Tours Cathedral.

The delightful grouping of Gerona's ancient glazing provides for us an ensemble upon which we shall often reflect with reminiscent satisfaction. Don't fail to stroll into the charming cloisters, whose quaintly carved capitals vie in interest with the picturesque view down upon the dashing river Guell far below.

FLANDERS

ALL readers know well that the Low Countries during the blossoming period of their stained glass (1576–1647) were provinces of the Holy Roman Empire ruled by the Spaniards Charles V and Philip II. But how may we best link the glass of those Flemish provinces to that of the Sovereign's country? What better for this purpose than the golden links of the Collar of the Golden Fleece, that ancient order of chivalry, than which none ranked higher in all Europe?

Nor is this suggestion so fantastic as at first it may appear. In nearly every church we shall visit for its windows in old Flanders—nowadays Holland and Belgium—there will appear somewhere upon the tinted panes the Golden Fleece insignia, indicating that the royal or noble bearer was the donor or that it was given in his honour. They were patrons of our delightful craft, were these grands seigneurs, which reflects as much credit upon themselves as upon the object of their cultured interest. We shall do well to remark that the higher these Knights of the Golden Fleece mounted the ladder of fame the more did they emblazon their distinction across stained glass windows. More windows were given by or dedicated to Charles V in the Low Countries than can be credited to any other wearer of the coveted insignia. These Knights were not only warriors of high renown (else they could not win the Collar) but were also connoisseurs of art, and as such they jealously guarded all and several the dignities appertaining to their distinguished brotherhood. This meant much attention to pomp and panoply. Hark to an account of the stately fashion in which they proceeded to a Chapter or meeting held November 29, 1431. At the head of the column marched twelve trumpeters, bearing the arms of the Founder, Philip the Good, Duke of Burgundy, followed by the Heralds of Brittany, Sicily, Orange, St. Pol, Namurs, Viane, Enghien, Zeeland, and the Kings-at-Arms of Berry, Brabant, Flanders, Artois, and Hainault, with fifteen poursuivants. Next in line are a body of two hundred gaily garbed mounted gentlemen. After these come sundry bishops and mitred abbots, attired in rich pontifical robes and attended by a

notable company of clergy. All these but whet
our interest in the next and most important division
of the pageant, consisting first of the Officers and
then the members of the Golden Fleece. On they
come, headed by their Chancellor, Treasurer, and
Greffiers, clad in red robes, mantles and hoods,
with fur on the robes but none on the mantles,
except that of the Chancellor. Then follow, two
and two, on magnificent steeds, the eighteen Knights
of the Golden Fleece, all eminent statesmen or
warriors, in vermilion robes reaching below the knee
and bordered with grey fur. Over these robes
hang long fur-edged mantles of fine scarlet cloth
richly embroidered with heraldic devices. Outside
this sumptuous raiment each knight wore the golden
linked Collar of the Order. These worthies were
followed by thirty Pages of Honour in gay attire.
Last of all came the Order's Chief and founder,
Duke Philip himself, attended by a goodly company
of his counsellors.

Brilliant as was this display, it evidently did not
content the distinguished statesmen and soldiers
who comprised its select body of Knights, for their
records show that embellishments were constantly
being added to the pomp and panoply of their

public appearances. For example, in 1473, Duke Charles the Bold, after formal approval voted in Chapter, decreed that the mantles and hoods be thenceforth of crimson velvet lined with white satin. The sumptuous details of these costumes are of especial interest to us glass-pilgrims, because if we know when the different changes were ordered, it helps us to date the glass. This tendency to develop the splendour of their attire reached a climax when Philip II, having succeeded Charles V as head of the Order, set such a high-water mark of magnificence that none could hope to surpass it. Let us turn to a contemporary account of a Chapter held under his governance in 1559 :

We are in Antwerp at three o'clock on the afternoon of the twenty-first day of January and eagerly awaiting the passage of the gorgeous company to its solemn session. Marching at their head comes a herald on foot, and after him surpliced clergy bearing crosses precede eighty-five priests in copes of cloth of gold, velvet and silken damask. Next come eleven monks likewise in copes of cloth of gold, then three abbots bearing crucifixes, a dozen in mitres and several bishops. Next on prancing steeds pass two hundred gaily apparelled gentlemen. After these, two golden columns are borne aloft, each on the shoulder of a horseman, who are escorted by a band of thirty-six mounted trumpeters, half in black and half in the King's colours—yellow velvet edged with red and white— and all of them trumpeting lustily. And now, the preliminaries over, four heralds, each bearing the royal coat of arms, make clear the way for the four High Officers of the Order, in crimson velvet robes lined with white satin. They are followed by the Knights of the Golden Fleece attired in all the magnificence that a century and a quarter of study could devise. Behind each Knight march on foot his gentlemen and liveried servants. After this gorgeous array of Knights and their retainers follow thirty Pages of Honour, all in yellow. Next in solitary grandeur and mounted on a noble charger rides His Majesty King Philip II. In his rear and closing the procession, are two hundred German and two hundred Spanish pikemen all in yellow, red, and white, their yellow bonnets set off by one red and one white plume, their hose of yellow for one leg and white and red for the other. A hundred archers in equally striking garb bring up the rear.

The Order of the Golden Fleece was founded January 10, 1429, by Philip the Good, Duke of Burgundy, on the occasion of his marriage to Isabella of Portugal. So the Iberian Peninsula is well to the fore at the very beginning of the Order's history. And the relations of the Low Countries with that distant Mediterranean land are to become closer and closer, as will appear not only in the history books, but also by the distinguished names upon the Order's roster, for there we shall see many royalties and nobles both Spanish and Portuguese. It is interesting to note that during the heyday of stained glass many other distinguished names of other lands where flourished our craft likewise appear upon the same roster. Four kings of England, Edward IV, Henry VII, Henry VIII, James I, and three kings of France, Francis I, Francis II, Charles IX, are there associated with many another sovereign of Portugal, Hungary, Bohemia, Denmark, Poland, Sicily, and princes, archdukes, marquises, and counts galore.

At first the Order was restricted to twenty-four with the ducal founder—" vingt quatre chevaliers de noms et d'armes et sans reproche, nés en léal mariage." In passing, we may remark that at least two of the Knights (Nos. 54 and 111) made no secret of their having been born out of wedlock, indeed they boasted of being the Bastards of Burgundy! The number of Knights was raised in 1516 to fifty-one with the approval of Leo X expressed in a papal bull.

The statutes promulgated by the founder required that the Knights should hold a Chapter at least once every three years, that it must take place within the choir of a church on St. Andrew's Eve (November 29th), and be followed by a mass on each of the succeeding two days. Many of these details were subsequently modified. One requirement, however, was long unchanged,—that at every Chapter a careful inquiry be held by the assembled Knights concerning the conduct of each of their number, even of the sovereign who presided, and these investigations were pitiless. Beginning with the youngest, each Chevalier in turn withdrew from the meeting lest his presence embarrass a full and free discussion of his behaviour, only returning after the vote of approval or the contrary. Last of all, the sovereign himself retired, and he was discussed with the same freedom as the rest. This we know from recorded criticisms of sovereigns voted on

184

certain acts considered blameworthy by their colleagues. Even so illustrious a member as Charles V did not escape their censure, for six remonstrances were voted against certain of his acts. In similar fashion, a Chapter rebuked Charles the Bold in 1473, and another Maximilian in 1481. In almost every case these criticisms of the Order's Chief were taken by him in good part. The only exception seems to be Philip II, for not long after a vote of the Chapter blaming him for spending too much time on his toilet, he obtained authority in 1563 from Pope Gregory XIII not only to suppress these inquiries and the necessity of holding Chapters at which they could be voted, but also to substitute appointment of new members by the sovereign for elections by the Knights in formal session. " He laughs best, who laughs last ! "

Between 1429, the foundation year, and 1559, there had been held twenty-three elections of new members. Of these members, a goodly number are depicted upon the windows of the Low Countries. Ten of these twenty-three Chapters were held under Philip the Good, two under Charles the Bold, three under Maximilian, two under Philip the Handsome, five under Charles V, two under Philip II, and almost all at some city within the territory now known as Holland or Belgium.

Philip the Handsome married Joan of Aragon in 1495, and in 1500 held his second Chapter of the Golden Fleece in Brussels, at which his six-year-old son Charles, later to be Charles V, was received into the Order. None of its members ever held it in higher esteem or did more to enhance its prestige than Charles. He was declared of age in 1514, and in 1519 was named Emperor of the Holy Roman Empire. It is an odd fact that a feature of the Coronation ceremonies of this distinguished connoisseur of stained glass should have destroyed much of it, for we read that discharges of artillery in his honour at Bologna broke many of the old windows in the Cathedral there.

This gallant warrior, a doughty knight in a time of frequent armed encounters in the lists, and 114th in order of election to the Golden Fleece, was a notable traveller, as became an Emperor of such wide domains. Nine times was he in Germany, six in Italy, ten in the Low Countries, four in France, and twice in England and Africa. He defeated his great rival Francis I of France in three wars, and won so many battles in so many lands as to make of their recital a tiresome business. Everywhere we travel to-day across the wide territories he governed we are struck by how frequently it is stained glass that records his pre-eminence. You have seen him thus at Seville, come with us now through the Low Countries to see him on many another window.

Because the Golden Fleece was founded in Bruges, it is logical to begin our Flemish tour in that city. Thirty coats of arms above the choir-stalls of Nôtre Dame commemorate a Chapter of the Order held there, and twenty-eight similarly placed in the Cathedral of St. Salvator indicate who attended the thirteenth Chapter held there in 1478. In Nôtre Dame there is still a fine window in the Chapel off the choir given by the de Baenst family. Its Renaissance architecture is quite elaborate, and so heavily coloured are the Virgin and Child at the centre and kneeling donors below as to hint at a German glazier of the 16th century. At the Cathedral an ambulatory chapel, the third on the left, has a much restored 16th century window.

In the Chapel of the Holy Blood (Saint Sang) are some modern imitations of 15th century glazing, three on the right side, six on the left. When in 1844 it was decided to replace early glass long since destroyed, the original drawings were found in the Chapter's archives, and followed by the modern glaziers. Would that modern restorations elsewhere had been carried out in the same spirit !

But it is in the charming little Jerusalem Church, only thirty feet wide by forty long, that we glass-pilgrims shall find consolation for the departed glories of Bruges glazing. Here is a series of six small windows, two each on the northerly, westerly, and southerly sides, commemorating the Adornes family so frankly that there is no pretence of adding biblical pictures. They begin on the north by a window piously devoted to the parents of the founder, followed by one to the founder himself, then one to his son, another to his grandson, etc.—an interesting pageant of the Adornes *patri familæ*, each with his wife and his patron saint—completely protected both in this life and in the one beyond ! In the lower quarter of each embrasure are five coloured coats of arms against a ground of yellow stain. The two to the south are dated 1560. The scenic backgrounds behind the kneeling donors are more laboriously treated than was customary

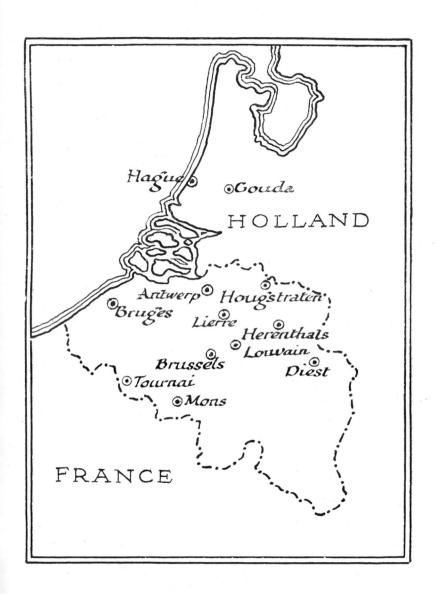

Hague

Gouda

HOLLAND

Antwerp

Hougstraten

Bruges

Lierre

Herenthals

Louvain

Brussels

Diest

Tournai

Mons

FRANCE

in the 16th century ; the fleecy white clouds are
leaded separately into the light blue sky instead of
being painted in.   Another unusual feature is that
the donors in the westerly window are facing due
easterly so as to be turned toward the altar, like
their fellows along the side-walls.   The Renaissance canopies above the figures are broken in the
Baroque manner.   Small as is this Jerusalem Church
its windows amply repay the two-hour train trip
from Brussels.

Because Bruges was the birthplace of the Golden
Fleece, we have perforce begun our tour at this city.
It must be admitted, however, that it would be more
practical for those arriving by motor or train from
France, Holland, or Germany to consult the
itinerary described at page 8.   If the pilgrim
begins from the Holland side, Gouda will be his first
point, but if he comes from France, he will probably
start his tour at Mons, and if from Germany at
Liège.   In any event he is sure to select either
Brussels or nearby Antwerp as a centre from which
to visit the other windows of the Low Countries.
There is here introduced a map to facilitate the
pilgrim's excursions.

GOUDA

IT is most fortunate for the renown of Dutch mediæval glass painters that they worked much abroad as well as at home, for " wars alarums " has played sad havoc with the windows in Holland. Alas! only Gouda preserves for our delectation any considerable display of their skill, but there, a great barn of a church proves to be one of the most delicious bowers of tinted light that has come down to us from the 16th century. Elsewhere there is little or nothing. The battling burghers of this land of dykes put liberty first and the preservation of things artistic a bad second, and certainly the invading Spanish overlords took no gentler stand. Patriots who were willing to bear every privation and even flooded their fields won so patiently from the sea, thought smashed windows but a small price to pay for outfighting the Spanish uitlander.

If we knew nothing else of Dutch glass painters than that high esteem abroad caused their frequent.

invitation to Spain and England, that would have been enough, but when we see what they there achieved, especially in Spain, we must rank them with the highest in their craft. Fortunately, Gouda can show us what they were at home and at their best.

The great church of St. John, said to be the largest in all Holland (300 feet long), would certainly never be visited were it not such a glorious Gallery of Glass. Its spacious but plain interior vaguely suggests the 'tween decks of a huge broad-beamed galleon rather than a place of worship. And this anchored galleon seems prepared to house a boxing match, because of the tiers of seats rising on all sides around the central space. It is a strange Dutch custom, this, of constructing an arena inside a church, with wide unoccupied space all around.

The extraordinary array of thirty-one great windows glazed in colour are almost all of six ample lancets, only a very few being of four or three. The best of them were done by the Crabeth brothers, Dirk and Walter, who earned such a reputation by their work here that they were summoned to Oxford to do the windows of several colleges, notably Wadham. It must be admitted, however, that nothing they did in England reached the standard

they set up in Gouda. The windows begin in
1555, then follow three in 1556, and next the
splendid one given in 1557 by King Philip II of
Spain and his consort, Queen Mary of England.
After these the dates run along down to the end of
the century, and a few follow on in 1601, 1603, etc.
Philip II's window modestly advises us in decorous
Latin that he is "the most illustrious son of the
most invincible Charles V," and that he is "King of
Spain, England and France, and both the Sicilies ;
Archduke of Austria ; Duke of Burgundy, Brabant,
Gelder, etc. ; Count of Flanders, Hainault, Holland,
Zeeland, etc." That is all, but it seems to us
moderns a fairly comprehensive lecture on
geography ! The way in which he and his queen
are introduced into the picture is both unique
and quaint. Dirk Crabeth makes them part of the
Last Supper group by placing them kneeling close
to the table ; facing them, and somewhat interested
in their appearance, is a dog ! Their crowns and
royal robes, and Philip's collar of the Golden Fleece,
contrast oddly with the homely garments of the
Saviour and His disciples disposed around ..e board.
Incongruous, even for mediæval glass donors, so
often incongruous folk.

Of course the architecture piled up by the artists on many of the windows is of the classical Renaissance type appropriate to the second half of the 16th century. Right next to Philip's window is one given by the Duke of Brunswick, but it might more fittingly be the gift of a guild of builders or architects, so overwhelmingly prominent is the two-storied, many-coloured palace that occupies most of its surface, stretching far back into the perspective.

The earliest window of all, given in 1555 by the Bishop of Utrecht, is in the church's eastmost embrasure. The donor has magnanimously consented to a 50–50 division of space between his own carefully drawn portrait claiming the lower half, and a many-peopled scene in the upper half showing John baptizing the Saviour in Jordan. There is no doubt about which half was of more interest to Dirk Crabeth,—he did not forget who was to pay him ! But worthy Dirk was not alone to blame for the pains he lavished upon the bishop's portrait in this window No. 15 ; in No. 18 he tucks the donors away in the bottom of the picture, where they are as modest in size as they are in placing.

Following on round the apse to the main body of the church, another lesson in geography awaits us at window No. 22, Christ casting the Money Changers out of the Temple. This was given by the Most Noble Lord, Prince William of Orange, Count of Nassau, Katzenelleboge, Vianden, Diest (where we shall find pleasing windows), Lingen, Buren, Leerdam, etc. ; Marquis of TerVeer, Noseroy, Castleballin, etc. ; Hereditary Viscount of Antwerp, Besançon, etc. ; Governor-General of Brabant, Holland, Zeeland, Vriesland, Utrecht ; Admiral-General of the Mediterranean Sea, and Knight of the Golden Fleece. What an unrolling of the map !

The window that gives the author the most pleasure of any in all the Low Countries is No. 25, setting out in engaging detail the relief of besieged Leyden. The dykes have been cut, and across the flooded country go boats without number, proceeding from Delft on the left out to beleaguered Leyden in the distant background. Also there is much fighting going on, so that spirited incidents in every part contribute to a most lively whole. The manner in which the large figures in the foreground balance the miniature groups in the background reminds one of Velasquez' skilful composition in his Madrid masterpiece " The Surrender of Breda," commonly called " the Lances," from the forest of them held aloft by the soldiery.

The quaintest of the entire Gouda series are the two three-lancetted lights, Nos. 30 and 31, near the western end of the church, and said to be by Dirk Crabeth's pupils. The former shows Jonah emerging from the spacious countenance of the whale, and was appropriately donated by the Company of Fishmongers ! In the latter, Balaam is beating his ass suddenly become conversational ; this, with small sense of humour, was given by the Company of Butchers. Especially complete is the Jonah picture, for not only is the large white whale receiving delivery of him from his ship back in the right background, but also, in the " close-up " of the left foreground, the enormous whale's head, stretching nearly the entire height of the embrasure, is facilitating the unhurried exit of an over-dressed Jonah, entirely unruffled by his stay in this primitive submarine.

THE HAGUE

ALTHOUGH The Hague (half an hour by train from Gouda, 28 kilometres by road) has not enough ancient glass to justify listing it with the towns that follow, nevertheless, if our pilgrims happen to be in the Dutch capital they should visit the Groote Kerk to see its two interesting 16th century windows. As we enter by the nave we shall see up on the south wall two long black boards that doubtless came from above the choir-stalls long since removed. Upon these boards are painted thirty coats of arms, each surrounded by a Collar of the Golden Fleece, commemorating the attendance of their owners at a Chapter of that Order held in this church in 1456.

In the eastmost embrasure of the apse is a window obviously dedicated to the greater glory of Charles V. Before a Virgin and Child (she trampling upon an ugly dragon) kneels the Emperor, imperial robes covering his golden armour, while upon his head is the crown of the Holy Roman Empire.

in Spain and Flanders

Near by upon the tesselated pavement lies his golden helmet, while behind him stretches a perspective of marble halls, so empty as to seem echoing. His device, Plus Oultre, is twice repeated above in the tracery lights, while below are set out all his titles, flanked by eight shields to right and left, of provinces of his empire. Here we have Aragon, Castile, Cordoba, etc., while oddly enough Portugal is thrice repeated.

In the north wall of the apse is another Renaissance window whose legend proclaims it a gift of the Collegium Canonicorum. Thirteen kneeling canons all in white, grouped about one of their number richly garbed who is upright, fill the lower third of the window. Just above them runs a narrow transom bearing their fourteen coats of arms in colour. The upper two-thirds contains an Annunciation with bright-hued figures, — Mary kneeling at the left before an angel on the right, above whom appears God the Father in a cloud. Charles V's device, Plus Oultre, is seen in the clouds that crowd the tracery lights.

Going by train from Gouda to Antwerp by Rotterdam requires three hours and a half because

197

of custom house delays at the frontier. By road it is 130 kilometres, but here also are delays, caused by the necessity of ferrying one's motor-car near Dordrecht from Willemsdorp to Moerdijk. If one goes south by Breda, Hoogstraeten, twenty-two kilometres beyond it, can be visited *en route* to Antwerp. Do not miss Hoogstraeten! From Rotterdam via Dordrecht and Breda to Antwerp is 110 kilometres.

HOOGSTRAETEN

NOT so numerous as the Gouda windows, but finer, much finer, are those filling the choir and transepts at Hoogstraeten— in fact, they provide one of the most beautiful ensembles of Renaissance glass anywhere to be seen. One has to go to King's College Chapel, Cambridge, to surpass it. On no account must a visit to Hoogstraeten be omitted. Not even Spain itself can boast a handsomer glazing tribute to the great Charles V than is here installed. That Emperor served both his own memory and also us pilgrims well when, in 1514, he raised the seigneurie of Hoogstraeten to the grade of a county in favour of Antoine de Lalaing, for the new count signalized the event by erecting a large church containing, mostly at his own charge, many fine windows around the choir and transepts and two elaborate ones at the transept ends. These last are not only lofty, but also spaciously broad, for below their roomy and elaborate traceries each has no less than eight wide lancets. The one in the north transept is even finer than that in the south, and its admirable Last Supper is full of interesting detail. The date, 1535, is two years later than the southern one. Its gorgeous pavilion frame with blue and green columns is perfected Renaissance at its best. Forming a sort of portrait gallery below the great picture stand eight Counts of Holland, distinguished representatives from a long line, with Thierry the First, who in 863 Charles the Bold made the first Count of Holland, and ending with Charles V himself, who had this title amongst so many others. A golden shield charged with a red lion hangs by green ribbons from each count's hand. In our study of 16th century Spanish glass we have noticed the use of reds in the Renaissance canopies, and in Flanders also this sometimes occurs. It is to be found here in the south transept window, but in this northerly one blue, a strong blue, is used in exactly the same manner, which is exceedingly rare. Of course the Collar of the Golden Fleece is here very much in evidence. This gallery reminds one of the English Kings in the Coventry Guild Hall. Note the carefully drawn landscape forming the background in both the upper and the lower half of this window.

HOOGSTRAETEN
Spanish Renaissance at its fullest development. One of the most elaborate glass
pictures in the world, and among the very finest

Across to the south the Circumcision and the Adoration of the Magi (1533) divide the whole space between them, for here we have no gallery of historical personages as opposite.

These transepts are rather short, being only two bays long. As at Avila Cathedral the embrasures all along the western side of the transept are bricked up, perhaps to avoid overlighting. The east side transept windows, dated 1537, 1539, 1548, are so much restored as to be almost modern, and one of them is entirely so, but they harmonize agreeably with their more completely ancient neighbours.

The best of the eleven windows around the choir is the eastmost one (1537), and it is the only one entirely given over to Biblical subjects. Above is a scene representing Penitence, and below is Our Saviour giving His Life on the Cross for sinning humanity. The background of the latter is an admirable landscape, a feature common to many of this series in their upper half (Marriage, Extreme Unction, and other sacraments), while below are kneeling donors or patrons. Charles V himself appears on the one just to the left of the centre (1532), attended by his patron saint Charlemagne as at Brussels) ; about the blazon of Empire hangs the Golden Fleece's Collar. Other dignitaries are Emperor Ferdinand of Germany (Charles' brother) in window No. 2, Isabella of Portugal (No. 5), Philippe le Bel and Margaret of Austria (No. 6), while below in No. 7 is our benefactor Antoine de Lalaing himself, with the highly prized Collar. There are eleven windows in all around the choir, of which the seven eastmost were given by Count de Lalaing. The six most westerly embrasures, although reaching up as high as their neighbours to the east, only come down one-third as far as they do. The Renaissance minarets that cap all this series are thrown out in bold relief by the rich blue of the backgrounds. Effective use is made of green garlands bound with red ribbons woven in and out of canopies gay with golden stain.

We have to thank Count de Beauffort for his admirable restoration of these windows in the middle of the 19th century. The Lords of the Manor in many another locality would do well to emulate his laudable example.

If one is motoring down from Gouda to Antwerp via Hoogstraeten, a short detour will enable us to see the glass at Lierre in the church where Charles V's parents were married. To do this, instead of running Hoogstraeten-Oostmalle-Antwerp (35 kilometres) we run Hoogstraeten-Oostmalle-Lierre-Antwerp, which adds only 13 kilometres.

LIERRE

FOURTEEN kilometres south-west of Antwerp lies the small town of Lierre, significant to those interested in Charles V, for here on October 20, 1496, were married his parents Philippe le Bel and Jeanne la Folle, called Mad Joan in English. In Antwerp we shall visit that dainty oratory, the Chapelle de Bourgogne, dated 1497, whose stained glass shows it was intended to honour the newly married pair. The history of Charles' parents is a strange and sad one, wherein politics, greed, and madness are inextricably interwoven. In January, 1505, they took ship from Flanders for Spain, but a storm forced them to put in at the English port of Weymouth. On the 17th of that month Henry VII had them as his guests at Windsor, but once there they realized that a trap had closed on them, and that they would not be permitted to leave until Philippe signed a treaty promising in marriage to Henry his sister Margaret, Duchess of Savoy, a rich widow. This he reluctantly did on February 9th. This treaty also contained a stipulation that Philippe's five-year-old son, Charles, should marry Princess Mary of England. And this youngster was later to be the great Emperor! After three months of polite captivity the royal pair and their child were permitted to depart for Spain. September 25, 1506, King Philippe died of drinking an iced beverage on a hot day. His widow, overcome with grief at the death of her handsome mate, went mad, and ever after insisted on taking his coffined remains with her wherever she went. This gruesome fact became widely known, but nevertheless Henry VII, baulked of his earlier marital plans, twice requested her widowed but richly dowered hand in marriage. Her father, Ferdinand the Catholic, refused both requests, and the poor lady died in 1555.

Philippe and Joan's marriage took place in the church of St. Gommaire, which is rich in windows, some 15th century, some early 16th, but the earlier are the more interesting. The fifth in the nave is perhaps the most valuable 15th century example left in Belgium, and shows the Virgin attended by the Holy Ghost as a dove, with many angels round about. In the four corners are the four beasts of the Evangelists. At each side kneel the donors with their patron saints, John the Baptist and Saint Barbara, and of course the usual family-glorifying coats of arms.

The 16th century windows are in the north transept, and their treatment throughout is similar— above a scene from Scripture, and below kneeling donors with their patron saints, plus the customary heraldry.

The best windows of all are the five around the apse, No. 3 being behind the altar. Here is glorified the House of Burgundy, for although the upper part of each three-lancetted embrasure bears a saint, the real purpose of the glazing appears in the central zone below, where kneel the various sovereigns attended by patron saints, with four tiers of gaily tinctured heraldry beneath. The first four windows show in order Philippe de Savoie and his wife Marguerite, Philippe le Bel and his wife Jeanne, Emperor Maximilian and his wife Mary of Burgundy, and the two lads Charles and Ferdinand, the former destined to become the Emperor Charles Quint. On the fifth appear the four sisters of the young princes. A noble galaxy indeed, and one is moved to wonder if a more charming form of memorial can anywhere be found.

The central four out of six lancets of the westmost embrasure on the north side of the apse clerestory have 15th century Gothic canopies about their saints.

Lierre suffered from the fighting around Antwerp, and the windows sustained many shot holes from bursting shrapnel. Thus far the glass has been repaired by filling the gaps with white, which is perhaps better than injudicious restoration.

A remarkable Jubé arch lingers in our memory, indeed one has to go all the way to the Madeleine at Troyes for a finer one.

Twenty-three kilometres to the east, at Herenthals, there used to be a number of trade guild windows in the church of St. Waudru, but only one remains, that given in 1528 by the Arquebusiers in honour of St. Anthony. The saint, effectively robed in black and white, occupies the central lancet, and is flanked in the outer ones by crossed arquebuses in yellow stain.

Lierre is 14 kilometres south-west of Antwerp

Stained Glass Tours

Hoogstraeten lies a little east of north from Lierre, 34 kilometres away through Oostmalle, and from Hoogstraeten, coming down again through Oostmalle, the road runs south-west, 36 kilometres, back to Antwerp.

ANTWERP

AS one of the great ports of Europe, and also one of its busiest marts of trade, Antwerp has for centuries been a desirable prize whenever the intermittent fever of war reached one of its periodical outbursts. There must not be forgotten the well-established point in English foreign policy that Antwerp in hostile hands would be a pistol pointed at England's heart. This seems equally well understood by whichever Continental power happens at the moment to covet the aiming of the said pistol with malice prepense. It is small wonder, therefore, that Antwerp has often been fought for, and even greater wonder that of its former wealth of stained glass so much remains to be seen to-day.

Many and beautiful as were the windows formerly tempering the light for a score of its churches, to-day it is only in Nôtre Dame and in St. Jacques that we shall find any considerable quantity of mediæval glazing.

Before visiting those two larger sanctuaries, let us repair to the dainty little Chapelle de Bourgogne mentioned at Lierre as having been prepared for Charles V's parents just after their marriage. The author obtained a hint of its existence from an ancient book, which said it could be found in a back court of a building on the Longue Rue Neuve. Now this street is really a long one, and there are not a few chapels thereon. Numerous inquiries had produced no results when finally there was encountered a kindly and learned priest who led me to No. 31, the house of a parishioner, Mademoiselle Beukelaer. She conducted us through her back premises and across a courtyard, pausing there to tell how on the approach of the Germans, she had thrust her silverware down into the flower beds, replanting the flowers above it. At the back of this courtyard there was an arched gateway leading to yet another court. A stairway led up to a small oratory above the gate, and here was the ancient glass! The oratory was only 11 feet wide by 20 long and 19 high, bowed at one end with three small windows, and having another light at the opposite end, all of two lancets. This single light contained an Annunciation, while at the bowed

end were St. Andrew (patron saint of the Golden
Fleece) and St. James, flanked by Philippe le Bel
and his bride Jeanne, and Don John of Austria,
all under Gothic canopies, with heraldic blazons
below all but the saints. On the side walls of the
chapel are painted genealogical trees, and among the
pendentives of the ceiling appears the date 1497.
Everywhere are the initials P and J of the royal bride
and groom. This charming little oratory was
built by John van Immerseele, chamberlain of
Maximilian, who in 1499 made him Markgraaf
of Antwerp. No daintier an old-world interior
exists anywhere in the Low Countries.

And now for the two larger sanctuaries of the
city. St. Jacques has been through evil days. It
was necessary for Charles V in March, 1535, to give
permission by letters patent for the sale of enough
of its property to relieve the church's financial
embarrassment and provide funds for its completion.
It was roughly treated by the Calvinists and again
during the French Revolution, so that little of its
old glass goes back further than the early 17th
century. The best example of that period is the
1626 window in the Chapel of the Holy Sacrament,
just off the south transept to the east. Count

Rudolf of Hapsburg is offering his own and a companion's horse to a priest and acolyte carrying the Last Communion to a dying person. One does not blame the kneeling donors below so much for their excessive size and Flemish placidity of visage as for their strong browns, which quarrel with the delicate softness of the varying greens in the picture above. Scattered through this upper part are various episodes of the story, the foreground figures large, while the other groups diminish with the perspective, until the most distant ones are Lilliputian indeed. The rocky landscape through which progresses the little company before and after receiving the horses would have delighted Albrecht Dürer. Interesting also are sundry lights in the marriage chapel, Christ carrying His cross (1644) in the apse, and a badly restored Visitation to the right of the altar in the Holy Virgin Chapel. The most discussed window is the one depicting the Last Supper in All Saints' Chapel, off the north side of the nave. The kneeling donors, who died respectively 1528 and 1538, occupy its lower third. Some writers call this a copy of Leonardo da Vinci's famous fresco, but this is of course absurd to anyone who knows that masterpiece. The colour is heavy but rich, and the drawing is distinctly clever. The second embrasure from the west in this row (1677) has a Circumcision, the coloured picture in the centre being thrown out in bold relief by the broad frame of grey and white baroque architecture unusual because nowhere brightened by the usual touches of golden stain.

At the Cathedral of Nôtre Dame, that splendid example of Flemish architecture at its best, we shall find many windows, gifts of Kings, nobles, burghers, and guilds. The corner stone marking the enlargement of this church was laid July 14, 1521, by that puissant monarch, Charles V, with much pomp and ceremony in the presence of his brother-in-law, the King of Denmark, the religious and civil authorities of the city, and sundry Knights of the Golden Fleece. It is therefore but natural that the insignia of that distinguished Order appears more than once upon the glass.

It is interesting to note that Henry VII, the Lancastrian, and his Yorkish wife Elizabeth, daughter of Edward IV, gave one of the large windows in the Chapel of the Circumcision which lies alongside the north transept to the east. It very properly bears the red and white roses united through their marriage after a bloody civil war named for those gentle blossoms. A neighbouring window was the gift in 1503 of King Philip I of Spain and his wife Joanna of Castile, and here again we see the Golden Fleece pendant against a blue ground high up in the tracery lights.

Perhaps the best windows in the Cathedral are the fourth and fifth from the west along the northern side of the nave clerestory. They face the noble carved wood pulpit, and must surely refresh the spirit of the preacher. They date from 1537, and show the Conversion of St. Paul and the Adoration of the Magi, with donors below each picture.

Over the northern portal is a large window bearing the portraits of Albert, Archduke of Austria, and his wife Isabella. The Archduke is wearing the Order of the Golden Fleece ; the date is 1616. The most easterly window in the south wall of the nave is the Last Supper done to a large scale and given in 1503 by Count Engelbert II of Nassau, who was Burgraf of Antwerp. Its central portion was much restored in the 17th century. The graceful disposition of sixteen coats of arms about it has very wisely been copied in the numerous modern windows along the nave chapels.

ANTWERP CATHEDRAL.   CHAPEL OF THE CIRCUMCISION
Given in 1503 by Philip I of Spain and his wife Joanna of Castile.   He wears Collar
of the Golden Fleece, also twice repeated above in tracery lights.   Note border of
16 armorial bearings, a feature frequently repeated in this church

These Nôtre Dame windows exhibit to a degree unusual for their epoch a decided vigour of composition and strength of colour. It is a pity that many of them have been so badly damaged, but perhaps in view of the embattled history of the city, we should be grateful that so much of the old glass has escaped unharmed.

Frequent trains connect Antwerp and Brussels, taking about three-quarters of an hour. By road it is 40 kilometres, running through Malines, which lies about half way.

BRUSSELS

FREQUENTLY and magniloquently as do the ancient windows of Flanders boast the glories of Emperor Charles V and his royal kinsfolk, no wider sway is anywhere claimed for him than the Latin inscription on the great north transept window in the Cathedral of St. Gudule which calls him " King of Spain and the Indies, ruler of Asia and Africa, Most Clement Prince of the Belgians." This certainly claims the whole world for his parish ! Another window, the fifth in the Chapel of the Holy Sacrament alongside the apse on the left, used to bear the same inscription, but to-day only the first four of the series of seven ample embrasures retain their mid-16th century glass. These four survivors have along their lower halves handsome Renaissance pavilions containing counterfeits of Emperor Charles' sisters, brothers-in-law, and brothers, and are all dated: John III of Portugal and Catherine, Charles' sister (1542), Mary of Austria, another sister (1547),

King Francis I of France with Eleonore the third sister (1540), and King Ferdinand I of Hungary, Charles' brother (1540). The south transept window (1538) shows King Louis of Hungary and his wife, Mary of Austria, who after his death gave the 1547 window noted above.

Upon the upper half of these four 16th century windows just described there is set out a strange tale of the 14th century. Here we see depicted sundry episodes of the sacrilege committed by a Jew who stabbed a Communion wafer with his poniard and was amazed to see blood flow. Circumstantial details of this sacrilege are carefully recorded in the church archives, and so are all the business items concerning the erection in expiation of this Chapel of the Holy Sacrament. These items throw a light upon royal munificence in the Middle Ages, and show that sovereigns did not always feel it necessary to bear the entire expense incurred in the manufacture and installation of the glass. For example, King John of Portugal provided but 300 florins of the 375 spent for the first window, Mary of Austria 300 florins out of 342 for the second, and King Ferdinand 300 out of 400 for the fourth. For the third, however, Francis I of France sent 400 florins through his ambassador residing at Mechlin, which ampler payment perhaps explains why his window is the best of the series.

Just here it is apropos to remark that when the royal brothers-in-law Francis and Charles fell out, and the arbitrament of war gave Charles the victory at Pavia with Francis as his prisoner, part of the ransom exacted was a certain clerestory window from the church of St. Jean at Troyes. Here is striking proof of how highly Charles esteemed fine stained glass. What comment it would have caused if the Versailles Conference had included sundry stained glass windows in the reparation payments required of the Germans !

High up around the five apse clerestory windows to the east again appear Charles V and his kinsfolk, in each case the kneeling personages in the middle with three tiers of gay armorial blazons below and brilliant banners above. Here we have Archduke Maximilian, King of Bohemia, and his wife Mary of Burgundy, Philippe le Bel and Jeanne de Castile, Emperor Charles V and his brother Ferdinand, Philip II and Mary of Portugal, and Philibert of Savoy with Margaret of Austria. It is supposed that all these sumptuous family portraits were the

ST. GUDULE CATHEDRAL, BRUSSELS

Charles V. window in north transept.   Admirable adaptation of Renaissance style,
affording well-lighted interior in northern city.   Note Golden Fleece insignia below
Imperial coat-of-arms in tracery lights

gift of Margaret of Austria, but the otherwise voluble church records are silent on this point. The colouring is strong and the drawing satisfactory.

The most engaging window here is the great one at the west end with its eight tall perpendicular compartments crowned by elaborate tracery lights. Across it is spread a picture of the Judgment Day, and a very busy scene it is ! The whole lower part is filled with numerous nude folk rising up out of a grassy green earth. The gaze of all is directed upward across a light blue sky to where in the midst of angel hosts is God the Father against an orange-yellow background, picked out by red-winged seraphim. The composition is perhaps more crowded than effective, but there is no denying its interest for the spectator.

Along the right or southerly side of the apse is a long chapel balancing that of the Holy Sacrament on the other side. Unfortunately, here the glazing is not so satisfactory. It dates from the second half of the 17th century (1658, 1664, etc.), and it would seem that the artist thought it his business to secure a " dim religious light " by the smearing on of opaque colour. These windows might be effective and appropriate down in the strong glare of a Spanish city, but here under northern skies they shut off too much light and only serve to accentuate how much more suitably glazed are their neighbours in the transepts and the Holy Sacrament Chapel.

DIEST

ALMOST due east of Brussels and 55 kilometres away lies Diest. It is about the same distance from Antwerp, running out through Lierre, but the road from Brussels is much better. Twenty-nine kilometres from Brussels on this road to Diest lies Louvain, a reminder of the *furor teutonicus*, and also a monument to Belgium's power of recuperation, for whole streets of fine new houses replace those destroyed in the centre of the town. Because of the said furor, there remains no glass to interest us in the great old church of St. Pierre, but in the hospital of Les Sœurs Hospitalières there is a room containing eight small 17th century enamelled panels, while along a nearby corridor are fourteen roundels dated 1420, 1421, etc., of white and stain, with narrow borders of red, green, and blue, the initials I.H.S. frequently repeated, and pleasing Latin lettering. Their position along the lighted side of the corridor or gallery

221

is reminiscent of a similar but far finer one at the monastery in the Val d'Ema near Florence.

When we arrive at Diest and stop before the church of St. Sulpice, we shall be struck by the sharp contrast between the deep brown stone of its exterior and the light grey stone used for the figures and their canopies which ornament the flying buttresses.

Of the ten ancient but much restored stained glass windows still preserved here the two notable features are the number given by guilds of tradesmen, and the fact that the half which is of late 15th century manufacture show white robes with gay linings, which attire hints at German influence. The other half of the windows are 16th century, two of them dated 1524, and one 1521. The shoemakers seem to have been the most generous of the guilds, no less than four being due to their munificence, although in No. 8 are associated with them the grocers, the tanners, and the druggists. No. 10 was given by the bakers and the millers, who are shown at work in two scenes on the lower part of the window, while scattered over its surface are various utensils of the two trades. To make trebly sure that every observer learns who are the donors, there also appear their patron saints, St. Martin with a mill, and St. Honoré carrying a scoop. On the fifth window, one of those given by the shoemakers, are their patron saints, St. Crispin and St. Crispian, each holding in one hand the instrument of his martyrdom and in the other a shoe or cobbling tool. These gifts of the guilds are in the chapels along the south side of the nave. Note in the sixth from the west three gentlemen all being immersed at the same time in one rather crowded baptismal font. The windows given by the nobility are along the north side of the nave, are all of the Renaissance period, and their donors all wear armour. Small predella scenes run along the foot of the embrasures. Sundry rich red curtains materially brighten these north side panels.

The even balance maintained at Diest between windows given by tradesmen and those from the nobility renders this sanctuary an ideal lesson in harmonious economics. Coats of arms gorgeous with heraldic device, over against humble utensils of the guilds—why should not such effective contrasts make for decoration as pleasing as it was politically wise ?

LIÈGE

WHEN the war broke out in July, 1914, the author was in Germany preparing a book on German stained glass. What a summer to have selected for such a pursuit ! My family and I were detained by the military authorities in Münster, Westphalia, from August 4 to 12, when we were permitted to cross the border into Holland. On August 4th the Münster papers announced in large headlines, " Lüttich gefangen " (Liège is taken), and they continued so to proclaim day after day, but on reaching The Hague we found that the German army was still held up before that gallant city, which provided the delay necessary to complete the mobilization of the French armies. This bit of modern history with its personal slant gave the author a peculiar interest in viewing the Liège glass, and a feeling that it should share in the respect that its stout burghers and their manly king have won on both sides of the Atlantic.

We shall have to visit the Cathedral of St. Paul, and the churches of St. Martin, St. Servais, and St. Jacques to see their considerable remains of ancient glazing, but there are also fragments in other churches.

Of St. Martin's Church it is enough to say that its thirteen lancets—seven in the choir and six in the transepts—have been damaged as much by restoration early in the 19th century as by earlier revolutions and other warlike distresses. Parts of one window have been joined on to another, angels' heads peep out at unexpected points, destroyed parts are frankly replaced with coloured lozenge panes, etc. Over the three lancets at the end of the choir are spread many armorial blazons. Of chief interest to us as showing interrelation with the Iberian peninsula, are the arms of the Duke of Portugal and of the Kingdom of Portugal, not lost to Spain until 1640. All these are of the first half of the 16th century, and several are dated. The three lancets at the end of the choir have scenes from the history of St. Martin. Following on we have one given by Count Florent d'Egmont, a man of many titles, among them that of Captain General for the Emperor in the Low Countries, and Chevalier of the Golden Fleece, as is indicated by the collar of that Order. The stained glass in the transepts is poor and the restoration worse.

The six windows at St. Servais show the Birth of Jesus, Adoration of the Kings, Resurrection, Ascension, Assumption, etc. They date from the last years of the 16th century, and are more fortunate in their modern restoration than their cousins at St. Martin's. The coats of arms are not ancient, but represent those who defrayed the cost of the 19th century repairs, which seems entirely appropriate. The colouring is rich.

The Cathedral, dedicated to St. Paul, has one fine and large window, in the end of the shallow south transept. On one of the columns of the lower right-hand picture is the date, 1530. A stone transom divides the upper six lancets from the lower six. One great picture, the Coronation of the Virgin, runs all across the upper lights. The lower ones contain two, the Conversion of St. Paul to the left, while on the right the donor, Jean Houten, Dean here from 1519 to 1539, kneels in white before an altar. Behind him is seated the patron saint of Liège, St. Laurent, in bishop's robes. In the background is the ancient city of Liège, surrounded by walls with round towers. In the scene of the Conversion of St. Paul, he is falling from his horse. Both these lower pictures are framed in elaborate Renaissance architecture, throughout which is a liberal use of red, just as there is in the framing of another Conversion of St. Paul window in a nave chapel of Seville Cathedral. Note the small rounded balconies above these two lower pictures, peopled with small folk, who give a pleasing animation to the whole.

In the upper half of the embrasure the painter shows an utter disregard for the perpendicular mullions, as his strangely concentric picture spreads over them all. A rather incongruous note is struck by the introduction of the Saviour in wilderness attire, whilst God the Father is represented in full papal panoply, triple tiara, etc. The three central figures are surrounded by a circle of blue clouds, and these by another of brownish seraphim wings, and then another of parti-coloured busts, while the outermost circle is of puffy dark blue cloudlets. It sounds rather horrid, but the effect is good.

The most interesting Liège windows are at

St. Jacques, and they suffered least of all from the
French invasion at the end of the 18th century. Five
lofty three-lancetted lights are stationed around the
apse, and on their left is added an even nobler pair
each of four lancets but built together. All are of a
double tier of lights, separated by a stone transom,
and culminating in handsome traceries above. This
great window, the first on the left, was the gift of
Count Jacques de Horn. We know that this
gentleman was reprimanded by the Chancellor of
the Order of the Golden Fleece for drunkenness at
the Chapter thereof held in 1516, so perhaps we
are not assuming too much if we consider the gift
of this glass as an expiation of his undue hilarity !
Be that as it may, the Collar of the Order appears
on the design. The two kneeling ladies are
Marguerite de Croy and Claude de Savoie, his first
two wives. They help us to date the window as
between 1514 and 1520, the dates of his second
and third marriages. His second wife died in
1528, and his third wife, Anne de Bourgogne, does
not appear on the window. Suppose a man desired
to give a window in expiation of drunkenness, what
more seemly decoration could be found than two
kneeling wives, proof of reiterated domesticity !

Much heraldry appears throughout, mute testimony to family pride.

By contrast with this ancestral vainglory its next neighbour is the gift of the " 32 bons metiers de la ville de Liège," represented by their patron saints. The finest of all is dated 1522, and dedicated to the Holy Trinity, a subject to which its construction in three lancets readily lends itself. In the upper half is a well-drawn and coloured Crucifixion.

TOURNAI

IF one is at Brussels and returning to Paris, there is a comfortable arrangement by which he can see both Tournai and Mons and yet reach Paris late on the evening of the same day. To do this one takes the morning train from Brussels to Tournai, a trip of less than two hours. This permits one to lunch at the excellent hotel across from the Cathedral, see the glass, and then motor 48 kilometres to Mons, where there will be ample time for the windows of St. Waudru before the Paris express arrives from Brussels, on board of which one then dines.

For a student of 15th century manners and costumes, the twenty-three ancient stained glass panels now installed in the two round-ended transepts of the Cathedral will prove a veritable museum of interesting details. They were formerly ranged along the choir aisles, but not so advantageously displayed as here, for there they were only a band of colour at the bottom of glaringly white windows which completely drowned them, while now they fit their embrasures so the only light that enters comes through their tinted panes.

The legends depicted with such faithfulness of quaint detail obligingly fall into two groups, half for each transept. Those in the north transept recount the separation of this diocese from that of Noyon, an ecclesiastical intrigue that dragged on a hundred years, engaged the attention of five popes, and involved many visits to Rome and the use there of much money and influence. It was a drab business, but of this no hint appears from the gaily tinted folk crowding the little scenes of papal audiences, visits to lesser church dignitaries, travels by road, etc.—all culminating in the delighted outpouring of citizens to receive at last in 1146 a bishop of their very own ! The veracious chronicler does not scruple to show a golden purse from time to time, but " all's well that ends well," and the tedious and unsavoury struggle is happily crowned in the last of the ten panels. The first seven are in the lower portions of the embrasures on the left of St. Andrew's altar, and the three last in their upper parts, so that from the middle of the transept just in front of the altar, one sees them all at once.

Stained Glass Tours

Three of the scenes, the fourth, fifth, and sixth, show audiences with a pope, and here the costumes are especially gorgeous. In the eighth we have the King of France in purple robe bordered with ermine surrounded by much pomp and circumstance. In No. 10 are two contrasting groups, one of clergy, the other of magistrates, all intent upon officially confirming the new bishop's position by the sworn allegiance of the city authorities. Notice the rich reds and gold in the three papal audiences. Nos. 3 and 7 show life on the highway, and have an ample complement of horses and dogs.

Quite different is the story told by the glass across in the south transept. Here is no concealed intrigue but a straight-out business-like account of how when Chilperic, King of Soissons, defeated in 578 by his brother Sigbert, King of Austrasia, was given refuge by Bishop Chrasmer in Tournai, his wife Frédégonde hired two assassins to kill Sigbert, so that Chilperic emerged victorious after all. As a royal appreciation of the bishop's aid in time of sore need, he was granted certain rights and privileges to tax. Below on each window are historical episodes beginning with the defeat of Chilperic by Sigbert in single combat, his flight, the

232

queen hiring the assassins and their bloody deed, and finally the acknowledgment of the royal grant by the Bishop and the Provost. These panels tell their story in vivid fashion, but to us moderns that story (a droll defence for the divine right of kings !) is nothing like so interesting as the panels in the upper half of the same embrasures. There we have a detailed disclosure of each tax, and of how it was collected.

Modern legislators are supposed, before imposing a new tax, to investigate how it will work when put into operation. Here may be studied not one but five distinct and separate taxes, viz. that upon crossing a bridge, upon weights, wine, markets, and beer, and all appear to be working smoothly. The tax collectors are always priests, and generally treated with courtesy by the taxpayers, if one may judge by doffed caps, etc. There is no relation between the historical scene below and its tax-gathering companion above, except in the case of the fourth window. There we have in the upper half two priests collecting a wine tax in cash and in kind. Below is Queen Frédégonde seated on a throne making her murderous bargain with the two assassins ; here again we have both

233

cash and wine—a purse to pay the villains and wine
to encourage them. These panels are brightened
by the use of much red and gold. An effective
blue appears in the floating cloaks of the pursuing
horsemen and also in the golden-guyed tent within
which Sigbert is done to death. The small groups
at the back of several of these scenes repay attention.
Note the flattened beer kegs drawn on pull-barrows
without wheels. Nowhere is there any hint that
the cowardly murder for hire of one king by another
was anything but good business, indeed much care
is taken to show the profit both to the city and
Chilperic. May we claim that the standard of
public and governmental morals is better in these
latter days—or will many episodes of the late war
show that mediæval morals differed from ours only
in being franker ?

The oldest glass in the Cathedral is in the eastmost chapel on the south side of the nave, where
three four-lancetted windows have upon their middle
pair of lancets 14th century figures under canopy
against a blue or deep red damask background.
St. Barbara is the quaintest of them ; her companion
saint wears a red halo.

The only 16th century window here fills the east

side of the second chapel along the right of the apse ambulatory. It is dated 1526, and is a triumph of simulated architecture, whose golden stain aids the red of the costumes to make of this a brilliant ensemble. The other two embrasures of this chapel, on the south and west, are modern glazed but in harmony with their elder brother. Across the seven lancets of this great window run gallery above gallery, each differently treated, and one with a blue sky background. The Virgin with the Child, four angels holding her robe, fills the upper centre. To left and right are kneeling donors, a Pope supported by sundry clergy, and Charles V attended by a French King in blue fleurs-de-lys robe. A most effective piece of glazing, and unlike anything seen elsewhere in Belgium.

MONS

ONE of the most stirring stories of the late war is the spirited and dogged retreat across Belgium in 1914 by the first British contingents, since proudly styled "the Old Contemptibles," to have fought with whom is now a priceless heritage. That retreat was one long uninterrupted rearguard action, and fighting is discouraging business when any advance is known to be impossible. One of the bitterest struggles of this long-drawn-out battle took place when the British fell back through Mons, fighting every foot of the way. Naturally, it was only fair to assume that all ancient glass in that town was destroyed during that struggle. Nevertheless, to make assurance doubly sure, the author wrote the priest in charge of the church of St. Waudru, inquiring if by chance any of his old windows had survived. The courteous reply was signed Prince Ferdinand de Croy, who proved to be both curé and dean of that church. He gave reassuring accounts of the glass's condition, thanks to restoration conducted in both artistic and reasonable fashion, doubtless due largely to his intelligent interest and that of his brother Prince Henri de Croy, who lives with him. Poor Belgium ! so often has it been fought over during its own or other people's quarrels as to be resigned to believing that wars must come once in so often, like the cycle of a comet !

The church of St. Waudru is remarkable in that although it took more than two centuries to build, no departure from the original plan was permitted, so that the finished edifice is what the original architect contemplated when set to work in 1450 by Philip the Good, founder of the Golden Fleece. It is a roomy structure giving a bright airy effect. The contrast between the blue stone of the groining and the red brick of the vaulting is decidedly unusual.

There is no old glass in the nave, but around the lofty clerestory of the apse we shall find fifteen ancient stained glass windows of great size, while in the transepts five remain out of the original ten. These apse clerestory lights are stationed above an unpierced triforium which runs evenly all round the choir and also out around the transepts and nave.

The allotment of embrasures among would-be donors of their glass was carefully studied, and rank rigorously regarded. To the ducal family was awarded the embellishment of the eastern end of the apse above the High Altar, and along with them two distinguished clerics of the Croy family. The westerly choir windows fell to the lot of other nobles. In the transepts and nave were placed the windows donated by magistrates, clergy, and bourgeois. The upper portion of almost all these lights is devoted to scenes from Holy Writ, but ample space is always reserved below to acquaint observers with the identity of the donor, noble or priest or bourgeois, with considerable heraldic light upon his genealogy. In fact, we have here a veritable "Who's who" for this neighbourhood during the 16th century.

Let us first proceed to the easterly end of the choir to inspect its five eastmost clerestory lights, which are all of three lancets. In the first one on the left, dated 1440, is the Golden Fleece Collar ; among the blazons is that of distant Granada. No. 2, Jesus among the Doctors in the Temple, was given by Maximilian of Germany, as was also its next neighbour the central one, a Crucifixion.

MONS. ST. WAUDRU, APSE CLERESTORY

Philippe le Bel, wearing Collar of the Golden Fleece, as does also his son Charles (later Charles V); behind latter his younger brother Ferdinand. The same much-coveted Collar encircles Philippe's coat-of-arms above

In the latter we are surprised to find the Emperor and Philippe le Bel in the upper and not the lower part of the window, as was customary for donors. Again we have the Golden Fleece, this time with its Collar encircling the Austrian arms up in the traceries. The fourth embrasure has a special interest for those of us recently come from Spain, because it shows Prince Charles of Luxembourg, later to become Emperor Charles V. He and his brother Ferdinand kneel in the right panel before their father Philippe le Bel in the central one. Above are his arms, with the Collar of the Golden Fleece suspended above them. In the lower part of each of these windows are six brightly hued shields, three and three, and in all but the central one there are more of them above.

The remaining ten clerestory windows in the body of the choir are larger, the first on the right and left (gifts of the de Croys) are of four lancets, and the other eight have six lancets, the donor generally to one side balancing his patron saint on the other, with a Biblical scene between them. Here we have much depicted architecture, still Gothic, although we are now well on in the 16th century. The transition into the Renaissance or classical style is best shown on the fifth window, the Purification, given by Jacques de Croy, bishop and duke of Cambrai. On several of these windows we shall see the Golden Fleece.

Architectural borders are more frequent along the south side than opposite, but even here are many heraldic shields, so important a part of the decoration on the north side. Indeed, over there the third from the west has no less than 32 large coats of arms, each filling a square of its own, and providing an unduly wide frame for the picture of Christ in the manger occupying but one-ninth of the whole embrasure. All the westerly ten are 16th century except the second from the west, dated 1615,—its bright red columns and orange-yellow touches are too florid for the otherwise harmonious colour scheme of this splendid gallery of fifteen great windows.

Of the five ancient windows which remain in the transepts the best is the large one over the north porch. This was given by the City Fathers in 1522, and represents the death of the Virgin Mary, stretched on a bed holding a lighted candle and surrounded by Apostles, all within an elaborate Renaissance pavilion hung about with green curtains except for the deep red one at the head of the bed. Peeping down from two small windows above are two pertly bonneted youths,—a rather incongruous touch. Across at the other end of the transept is an entirely different type of glazing. There, Christ baptized by John covers the four central of eight lancets, with about it a thickly toned Renaissance frame. Up each side run seven panels of arms against grisaille.

An amusing legend comes down to us about window No. 9 of the choir clerestory. Here in this church a certain Buisseret performed an exorcism upon Jeanne de la Croix. The exorcised imp, in order to escape from the sacred precincts, broke out through this window, and the glass we now see was given to replace that which he broke. It is fervently to be hoped that departing evil spirits may in like manner break much of our modern glass, so that improved examples may be substituted !

Of more sinister memory, however, are the shot holes in many of the ancient panes, significant reminders of the 1914 fighting in the streets of Mons on a day when evil spirits broke in, and not out.

CHRONOLOGICAL TABLE OF GLASSMAKERS

15TH CENTURY

1418	Master Dolfin	Toledo.
1429	„ Luis	„
1439	Pedro Bonifacio	„
1459	Master Cristobal	„
„	„ Pablo	„
„	„ Pedro	„
„	Pedro Frances	„
1497	Juan de Valdivieso	Burgos and Avila.
1498	Juan de Santillana	„ „

16TH CENTURY

1503	Vasco de Troya	Toledo.
1504	Micer Cristóbal Aleman	Seville.
1509	Alexo-Ximenes	Toledo.
1510	Juan Hijo de Jacobo	Seville.
1513	Gonzalo de Cordoba	Toledo
„	Juan de la Cuesta	„
1518	Bernaldino de Gelandia	Seville.
„	Juan Vivan	„
1519	Juan Bernal	„
„	Juan Jaques	„
1520	Alberto de Hollanda	Burgos and Avila.

242

1522	Master Juan Campa	Toledo.
1526	Pedro Fernandez	Seville.
1534	Juan de Ortega	Toledo.
1535	Nicolás de Hollanda	Burgos and Avila.
1538	Arnao de Vergara	Seville.
1541	Jorge de Borgona	Burgos.
1542	Diego de Salcedo	Burgos and Palencia.
1548	Giraldo de Hollanda	Cuenca
1557	Arnao de Flandes	Seville.
1559	Sebastian de Pesquera	,,
1562	Cárlos Bruxes	,,
,,	Diego de Valdivieso	Cuenca.
1565	Diego Diaz	Escorial.
,,	Francisco and Hernando de Espinosa	,,
,,	Master Pellegrin Resen and his son Renerio Resen	Madrid.
1566	Ulrique Estaenheyl Aleman	,,
1569	Vicente Menandro	Seville.
1571	Master Galceran	Escorial.
,,	Juan Guash S.	Tarragona.
1574	Nicolas de Vergara el Viejo	Toledo.
1579	Octavio Valerio	Malaga.
1581	Arce	Burgos.
1590	Juan de Vergara	Toledo.

17TH CENTURY

1600	Antonio Pierres	Madrid.
,,	Diego de Ludeque	,,
1602	Diego del Campo	,,
1605	Jorge Babel	,,

243

Stained Glass Tours

From "Diccionario de los mas illustres professores de las bellas artes en España." Madrid, 1800.

A REQUEST

IF, gentle reader, the author has found favour in your sight, kindly advise him (at the address below the Foreword) of any Spanish glass not herein reported which you may discover in your rambles.

BY THE SAME AUTHOR.

STAINED GLASS TOURS
IN ENGLAND

With Sixteen Illustrations.

Demy 8vo.   7s. 6d. net.

MORNING POST.—"It is well written, and in a style which shows that the author really feels the attraction of the art he describes."

SPECTATOR.—"Mr. C. H. Sherrill has written a book which shows him to be not only a true lover of mediæval glass, but proves also his enlightened comprehension of its evolution and its changing style. 'Stained Glass Tours in England' is a popular guide to the best examples among the many fine windows remaining in this country."

DAILY TELEGRAPH.—"Mr. Sherrill is additionally happy in the grace and ingenuity with which he illustrates his study by snatches of history and gleams of anecdote. Not only a study in art criticism, but a panorama of the national life."

DAILY GRAPHIC.—"A volume which should accompany every archæologically-minded person."

STUDIO.—"The various itineraries he maps out for the reader strike one as being extremely well arranged, and apart from its undoubted charm the work should prove of very practical value as a guide-book."

BIRMINGHAM DAILY POST.—"Mr. Sherrill's enthusiastic appreciation of mediæval is soundly based upon considerable technical knowledge and a very wide acquaintance with the best existing examples."

WORLD.—"A most acceptable guide-book, as well as a valuable contribution to art history."

QUEEN.—"Altogether this is a very pleasant book, which should make many friends both for stained glass and for itself."

WESTERN MORNING NEWS.—"This volume deserves unstinted praise."

LONDON: JOHN LANE THE BODLEY HEAD LTD., VIGO ST., W.